Balti

Baltic Lenin

A JOURNEY INTO ESTONIA, LATVIA AND LITHUANIA'S SOVIET PAST

* * *

Keith Ruffles

BELFAST, UNITED KINGDOM

Baltic Lenin/Keith Ruffles. 1st ed.

ISBN-13: 9781530169399

ISBN: 1530169399

*To the endless skies and meadows of green
Where lies the heart of the Baltic.*

Acknowledgments

* * *

Thanks must go to the Peter Kirk Memorial Fund and in particular to Gilly King and David Peacock for their help and support in making this journey a reality; without their help it's unlikely that I would ever have been able to spend all that time gallivanting around the Baltics chasing statues and ghosts in the name of research.

I'd also like to offer a special thank you to Ilari, Mari, Margit, Kristīne, Vlad, Arminas, Vytis, Rasa, Klaudija, Kristina and Ruta for offering a weary traveller both a bed for the night and memories to last a lifetime. This story is their story.

Contents

Preface

* * *

TUCKED AWAY IN AN OBSCURE corner of south-eastern Europe is a place where statues of Lenin still stand proud, where the hammer-and-sickle motif of the Soviet Union adorns public buildings and where weapons smuggling, people trafficking and the drug trade comprise just some of its more dubious exports. Welcome to Transnistria.

Transnistria is without doubt one of the most peculiar states in the modern world. A thin strip of land wedged between Moldova and Ukraine on the banks of the Dniester River, Transnistria is the black sheep of Europe, officially recognised by no one but stubbornly clinging to its independence and its Soviet past. It's more than a little ironic, then, that it was the very collapse of the mighty Union of Soviet Socialist Republics (USSR) in the last decade of the twentieth century that led to Transnistria's painful birth.

Let me explain. As the Union faulted and crumbled along ethnic lines at the beginning of the 1990s the majority Romanian-speaking Moldavian Soviet Socialist Republic seized the opportunity to declare its independence, taking Slavic-majority Transnistria with it. With the imminent threat of unification with Romania looming the Transnistrian authorities, with the help of the locally-based Russian Fourteenth Army, waged a short and bloody war with their non-Slavic neighbours. The result? *De facto* independence, albeit unrecognised by any other nation in the world. To this day Transnistria, despite having its own parliament, military, police, postal system, currency, flag, national anthem and coat of arms, continues to be considered by almost all international observers as sovereign Moldovan soil.

This false independence has not proved easy for the *Pridnestrovian Moldavian Republic*, or "PMR" as it chooses to style itself; politically and economically isolated from the rest of the continent and with its existence almost entirely dependent on the continued presence of the Russian armed forces, daily life is precarious for the half million or so inhabitants. Unemployment and inflation are rampant and the average wage is well behind the levels enjoyed in Western Europe. And the population is slowly ageing, with young people leaving in their droves in the hunt for better opportunities elsewhere, chiefly in Russia. It would be fair to say that Transnistria enjoys a truly claustrophobic existence.

The PMR neatly encapsulates the kind of cultural divisions that have plagued Eastern Europe since that monumental shift in the global balance of power back in 1991. Just as with Yugoslavia and its traumatic breakup at around the same time, the removal of the unifying force of communism (and, some would argue, a pervasive and oppressive centralised regime) opened the proverbial ethnic can of worms. It often felt like the Soviet Union *was* Russia, and it was always tempting to use the two terms interchangeably—just as some today might confuse and conflate England and the United Kingdom, to the great chagrin of the Welsh, Scots and Northern Irish. In fact the USSR was a vastly diverse place, and throughout its existence the gigantic nation had to keep a lid on these competing identities and simmering hostilities for the greater cause of socialist unity.

The regime's downfall led to the removal of that lid, and all the evils of cultural conflict boiled over. In some places the transition from Soviet republic to independent statehood occurred relatively peacefully, but in others—such as Transnistria—the result was all-out war. Atrocities and accusations of ethnic cleansing became commonplace as competing nationalisms fought over ownership of highly contested land. In the decades since, armed hostilities in Ukraine, Georgia, Tajikistan and the fractured republics of the Caucasus have all dominated the headlines, but in many more places the end of active hostilities did not mean that any adequate or satisfactory conclusion had been reached. These are the so-called frozen conflicts of the former Soviet Union.

I've always been fascinated by ideas of identity and nationalism, by the fact that men and women were willing to commit the most unspeakable horrors in the name of cultural defiance. It always seemed faintly ridiculous to me that things that none of us has control over—our place of birth, the language we speak or the accent we have—can define both how we view ourselves and how others choose to view us. This idea that I would, nay *should*, have more in common with a rich banker or a politician simply because we were both born in an arbitrarily defined geographic area than with someone else from another country with identical interests just made no sense to me, and yet here were people willing to give their lives and take the lives of others for the sake of a flag.

I was still a child when the Soviet Union disintegrated, and perhaps it was because of my age at the time that the process left a lasting impression on me: I might not have been old enough to comprehend the significance of these absolutely momentous events, but I could certainly empathise with the suffering of the countless victims beamed nightly into our television screens.

This book is really an extension of that interest. I visited Transnistria shortly before setting foot in the Baltics, and the shock and surprise of witnessing scenes of daily life that I thought had been consigned to the history books made me curious to know if other parts of the former Soviet Union were similarly affected—and maybe even in those places that are now part of the European Union.

Was it really possible that after such a long period of time the ghosts of the USSR could still be felt from beyond the grave? Were Lenin and Stalin still watching, keeping a careful eye on lands that had (in some cases for centuries) formed part of the greater Russian state? And would these places ever come under the orbit of Moscow again, just as they had for so long in times past?

I hope that you find reading this book as interesting as I found travelling around the Baltics. It is a fascinating, beautiful and utterly bewitching place.

CHAPTER 1

Boats and Statues

✳ ✳ ✳

THERE WAS A PARTY ATMOSPHERE aboard the packed ferry;
though barely nine in the morning, small groups of men
and women were already sipping from cans of weak beer
as their noisy offspring ran amok between decks. Some of
the older passengers quickly retired to the onboard restaurant, while others sidled up to some of the ship's numerous
game machines, emblazoned with names like "Gold Rush"
and "Treasure Island." The dollar signs flashed bright in
staccato yellow.

I decided to give these Bacchanalian delights a miss
and instead headed out on deck. The sea air was bracing,
rippling the waters of the Gulf of Finland as an unseason-
ably warm April sun glinted and gleamed on the waves that
lapped against our boat. I took a deep breath and looked
back towards a receding Helsinki, the city floating on the
horizon like some half-forgotten dream.

We were heading for Tallinn, capital of the Republic
of Estonia. It's a modern city with a medieval heart, the

soaring spires of its Old Town visible long before the rest of its buildings slid into view. As the ship glided into the dock we disembarked into glorious sunshine and strolled effortlessly through customs; no border guards, no passport checks. The majority of the ship's passengers—day-tripping Finns—had no need to hide their beverages.

Yet it wasn't always thus. When I was born back in the winter of 1982, the year of such seminal events as the Falklands War and the release of Michael Jackson's *Thriller*, the political climate was very different indeed. Estonia was not an independent country but the Estonian Soviet Socialist Republic, an integral and inviolable part of the Soviet Union. Communist Party leader Leonid Brezhnev was not long in his grave and the short rule of Yuri Andropov had just commenced. The Era of Stagnation, of near-terminal economic and social malaise, was truly at its zenith and Tallinn was just another Soviet town all but closed to curious foreigners.

Things are very, very different now. Estonia is an enthusiastic member of the European Union and NATO, having joined both organisations with its Baltic cousins Latvia and Lithuania in 2004—the first (and thus far only) members of the former USSR to do so. Indeed, Estonia led the way by adopting the euro, even as financial crisis raged across the Continent, an example that so impressed its southern neighbours that they also signed up to the eurozone shortly afterward. It would seem that Estonia has firmly thrown its lot in with the West.

The Old Town was lovely, a warren of medieval streets and alleyways that seemed little altered from the days when this was an important Hanseatic port, the powerful league of merchant guilds which dominated medieval maritime trade in northern Europe. Then known as Reval, the town made its fortune from the web of trade routes that criss-crossed the Baltic Sea.

And yet paradoxically it was never intended to be an Estonian city. Originally founded by King Valdemar II of Denmark in 1219, its heyday took place shortly after-wards under the auspices of a group of Germanic Teutonic Knights known as the Livonian Order. Subsequent post-Reformation weakness led to increasing Swedish domi-nation before the city's eventual incorporation into the Russian Empire in 1710 by the all-conquering Peter the Great, architect of beautiful Saint Petersburg. For almost the entirety of this period, Estonians constituted a minori-ty of the city's population but were still denied full citizen-ship rights; German would remain the language of social advancement right up until the First World War.

Things only really changed with industrialisation. The arrival of the railways in 1870 and the modernisation of the economy attracted more and more workers from the countryside, until Estonians finally formed a majority by the dawn of the twentieth century and thereby making the city the focus of an increasingly vocal nationalist move-ment. It would be here that the drive for independence would be most successfully galvanised by the chaos of the

Russian Revolution, and in 1918 Tallinn became the capital of an independent Estonia for the very first time.

Soon I found the place that I was looking for, on one of Tallinn's most touristy streets: an Indian restaurant, complete with street-side tables, chairs and parasols. It wasn't long after midday but already the place was doing a brisk lunchtime trade, the delicious smell of hot spices wafting over me as I opened the door. A few customers were eating cross-legged in spacious booths set into the windows.

One of the waitresses spotted me as the doorbell chimed my arrival. "Ah, you must be Mari's couchsurfing friend!" she beamed. I asked how she had guessed, winking as we both acknowledged the incongruously bulky rucksack on my back. "She's in the kitchen. Just grab a seat and I'll go find her."

After a couple of minutes Mari appeared. "Hello! Welcome to Estonia! It's good to see you!" she said, giving me a huge hug as I stood up to greet her. It was the first time we'd met and yet I already felt that we were good friends. She looked as lovely as her picture: piercing green-blue eyes, warm smile, dark-blond hair and a horrendously unflattering uniform. Welcome to Estonia indeed, I thought.

Late into the night of 23 August 1939 the foreign ministers of Germany and the Soviet Union sat down around a table and signed one of the most infamous treaties in modern history, the eponymous Molotov-Ribbentrop

Pact. In addition to promising that the two nations would not go to war in any upcoming conflict, a secret protocol declared that a vast swathe of Eastern Europe (including the Baltic states) would be divided into respective spheres of influence. In exchange for allowing Hitler a free hand in Poland Stalin would be able to reassert control over Estonia, Latvia and Lithuania—former Russian *governates* that had known independence for barely two decades.

The occupation came gradually. At first the USSR demanded that its forces be permitted to establish military bases in the Baltic, a demand to which those countries meekly complied. By the summer of 1940 the Soviet Union felt confident enough to occupy the Baltics outright; fixed elections—not-so-subtly supported by visible increases in Red Army personnel—produced predictably pro-Soviet governments that then obediently petitioned Moscow for formal incorporation into the USSR.

This first period of Soviet rule would last roughly a year and was characterised by mass arrests and deportations. Estimates vary, but it's generally accepted that at least thirty thousand Estonians, Latvians and Lithuanians— and perhaps as many as one hundred thousand—were packed up in trains and sent to camps in Siberia and elsewhere. Status afforded no protection; around a dozen current and former heads of state and some eighty ministers were exiled, executed or conscripted. Many of those who survived the war would not be permitted to return until the Khrushchev era of the 1950s and 1960s; even now some speak of a contemporary demographic deficit as a direct result of this policy.

All this changed when the launch of Operation Barbarossa saw Germany quickly invade and overrun the Baltics in July 1941. Initially welcomed by many as liberators, the Nazis successfully rolled back the Soviet forces and set up the Reichskommissariat Ostland, a sort of hybrid military-civilian government not dissimilar to those that had been established in other areas under Nazi control. Special units tasked with the extermination of Latvia's and Lithuania's considerable Jewish populations soon arrived, often aided and abetted by local collaborators. Ghettos were created in cities like Vilnius and Kaunas, and death camps operated openly on Baltic soil; in Lithuania alone around 90 per cent of the pre-war Jewish population was exterminated.

By 1944 the war had swung back in the Soviets' favour, and the Red Army once again swept victoriously through the Baltics. A curious and bitter three-way fight developed; German SS legions comprised of local volunteers were formed alongside regular units, while opposing communist sympathisers joined the advancing Soviets. Other disparate nationalist groups opposed to both formed a ragtag partisan movement known as the "Forest Brothers," fighting a guerrilla campaign that would continue well into the 1950s. It wasn't unknown for members of the same family to be pitted against one another.

At war's end Estonia, Latvia and Lithuania were devastated. Hundreds of thousands of people had been killed or deported or had fled abroad, national infrastructure was all but destroyed, and society was deeply traumatised and divided. Moreover the Baltics had been reincorporated back into the USSR—and would remain as such for another forty-five years.

I was sipping a hot chocolate in a café in Tallinn's trendy Coca-Cola Plaza when my phone rang. "Sorry I'm late!" blurted a heavily accented female voice down the line. "I'm just finding somewhere to park. Give me five minutes."

Exactly five minutes later Valeria hurried in. She spotted me right away and came over, joining me at the small table and immediately launching into conversation without pleasantries or introduction. She was a researcher at the University of Tartu, and her blond hair and Slavic looks betrayed the fact that she was a member of Estonia's minority Russian-speaking population. She was keen to talk about the status of the Russian language in Estonia, and I listened intently as I stirred my beverage.

"There is a big division between Russians and Estonians in Estonia," she said, looking straight into my eyes in a manner that was both authoritative and slightly unnerving at the same time. "We are like two separate communities, living separate lives."

"In what way?" I asked, slightly taken aback by this lack of conversational foreplay. It would seem that our previous e-mail exchanges over the past few weeks had already served that purpose.

"Well, things are easier now than they were in the 1990s. Then there was a lot of uncertainty, but some of that still remains. We celebrate completely different events. It's like we have differing interpretations of history."

I wondered what she meant by that. I asked her about the city's Museum of Occupations, created in 2003 to document life during the Soviet era. She grimaced.

"These museums are politically motivated: everyone knows that they are not a fair reflection of events as they happened. Look"—she leaned forward and stared at me even more intently—"Russian speakers do not share the same standards of living as Estonians. They often have lower incomes and cannot hold positions of authority. Okay, I know a lorry driver who's perfectly bilingual. His Estonian is perfect. He applied for a job and was successful. What happened? They saw his name, a Russian name. Then the offer was taken away. Estonians always have priority; it's always like this."

"Why is that? Why would they do that?"

"It has to do with narratives. In Estonia after independence, people rejected anything that reminded them of Soviet times. Russians speakers were marginalised for that reason, as if they were still Soviets—as if they were one and the same thing."

The thorny issue of "alien citizenship" is often cited as an example of this policy in action. When Estonia and Latvia—states with a large proportion of ethnic Russians— became independent they refused to offer full citizenship either to people who had emigrated from elsewhere in the Soviet Union after 1945 or to their descendants unless they could demonstrate a predetermined degree of proficiency in Estonian or Latvian respectively. To this day those who cannot pass the test are unable to vote and must use an "alien" passport, which denies them visa-free travel within the European Union. Some regard a reciprocal waiving of visas for aliens visiting Russia to be small consolation. It made me wonder whether these marginalised Russian speakers would feel any sense of nostalgia for the Soviet period.

"Oh yes, absolutely. I have one young student who thinks of the Soviet Union as a happy time when everyone was laughing and smiling. When I asked him why he thought this, he said he knew this from watching old films. It's a bit like how Estonians hark back to our first period of independence as some beautiful era when everything was perfect and there were no problems. Or Russians, for that matter."

"Perhaps it's this nostalgia that makes the authorities so suspicious. And what about the Bronze Soldier and Bronze Night? What does that event say about Russian speakers in Estonia?"

Valeria sat back slightly, looking a little sad. She bore the mildly exasperated look of someone who'd been asked this question before.

"Look"—that word again—"any Russian affinity to the Bronze Soldier is not a wish for the Soviet Union to be recreated, even though a lot of people think this is the case. For us it's about Russian dissatisfaction with our situation in present-day Estonia. We know the USSR will not return but we want to be full citizens, with the full rights that that entails. Isn't it natural to want this? Isn't it fair?"

Bronze Night was an event that shocked Estonia and finally brought the issue of the country's Russian speakers to the attention of the world's media. In April of 2007 the Estonian authorities declared that they would remove a controversial statue from the centre of Tallinn. This statue, the "Bronze Soldier," is a Soviet-era World War II memorial that for many Estonians symbolises the occupation and repression of the Soviet years. For many of Estonia's Russians, however, it represents not only the defeat of fascism in the apocalyptic Great Patriotic War (as Russians refer to World War II), but also their right to full participation in Estonian society—a blood sacrifice that saved the Baltics from the Nazi menace.

Rumours started to circulate that the statue faced imminent confiscation, sparking off two nights of violent rioting which resulted in one death, dozens of shops looted, and hundreds of arrests. A panicky government ordered the statue to be taken down immediately, placing it in temporary storage before finally deciding to deposit it in the military cemetery several miles from the centre of town, where it now stands.

It was only a short distance from the café to the cemetery but Valeria drove like the wind, covering the distance in only a few terrifying minutes. It was early evening, and no one else was around in the fading twilight. From the entrance a wide path led us past rows of well-maintained graves straight to the Soldier. It was an unmissable sight, completely dominating the area: a weary combatant in military fatigues, head bowed and helmet in hand, standing between plaques inscribed in both Russian and Estonian. Flowers and lit candles lay at the statue's feet, and although the monument was in the typically heroic style of the Soviet period it conveyed, at least to me, an air of sadness and regret.

I mentioned this lack of triumphalism to Valeria, who agreed enthusiastically with several nods of the head.

"This monument is a monument to everyone—not just Russians," she said. "See, even the soldier looks Estonian."

I couldn't really tell what the soldier's ethnicity was, to tell the truth. I did know however that it was less than a fortnight to Victory Day—the annual event marking the end of the Second World War—and I asked Valeria if she would be attending.

"Yes, of course. I come every year. It's important to me as a Russian speaker to go. It is where we go to remember our past."

"So will many Estonian speakers be attending?"

"No, of course not: that would be ridiculous. I told you before—we celebrate separate events. Not together."

We continued to stare silently at the bowed soldier for a few more minutes before deciding to head back to the car. It was a poignant introduction to this divided land.

After the end of the Second World War and the successful absorption of the Baltics into the Soviet Union Moscow-trained *apparatchiks* (Communist Party bureaucrats) were brought in to run the show, and a fresh round of deportations in 1949 served to remove the local intelligentsia and undermine nationalist aspirations. Operation Priboi ("Coastal Surf") saw an estimated ninety-five thousand people deported; in Estonia alone some 2.5 per cent of the population was sent to camps in Siberia and elsewhere.

The aforementioned Forest Brothers, meanwhile, continued their activities in the hope that help from external sources would eventually arrive; many received training in the West before being covertly transported back to the Baltics. Reprisals were bloody and fierce, the Soviet authorities executing many of the partisans they captured and frequently putting their bodies on public display to act as a warning to others. But help would never come, and the fragmented movement eventually died out after a spate of amnesties in the post-Stalin thaw of the mid-1950s—although a few solitary activists continued the struggle for years afterwards.

Yet life in the Baltics during the Soviet period was by all accounts relatively stable, if a little stagnant; political freedoms were tightly controlled, and even those Communists who questioned the centralised and Russian-dominated state were often purged. Industrialised Estonia and Latvia also experienced a substantial change in their ethnic composition as workers from all over the USSR flocked to the region, encouraged by a regime keen to maximise production. It's this migration which largely accounts for the high proportion of Russian speakers in these countries today; largely agrarian Lithuania, in contrast, never attracted incomers in such numbers and to this day remains more culturally homogenous than the other Baltic nations.

Despite these restrictions the standard of living in the Baltics was relatively high, especially when compared to the rest of the Soviet Union, and the authorities even permitted certain aspects of native culture to flourish; music in particular provided an outlet for nationalist sentiment. In hindsight it's perhaps no surprise that it was here, on Baltic soil, that Gorbachev's twin policies of *perestroika* and *glasnost* sowed the seeds for the USSR's ultimate demise.

CHAPTER 2

Eastern Promise

* * *

WHEN I WAS SEVEN MY dad took me to a stamp exhibition in London. This was no ordinary expo, however; this was Stamp World 1990 at London's Alexandra Palace, a celebration of the 150th anniversary of the very first postage stamp in the world: the beautiful Penny Black.

It was fantastic. There were stamps from all over the globe, from countries and territories and other places I'd never heard of. There were triangular stamps, stamps with advertisements on the back, stamps with which you had to use glue to make them stick to the envelope, and stamps that were more like stickers. I was instantly hooked.

As a small boy I quickly learned that the beautiful thing about stamps is that they can transport you to distant lands from the comfort of your own cluttered bedroom. I travelled wide-eyed all over Europe, to colonial Africa and India, to tiny Pacific islands and the farthest regions of the Far East. I encountered kings and queens, exotic animals and mythical beasts—stories told of countless countries and empires that have been and gone. It was a great way to travel.

By sheer coincidence, not long after I attended that stamp exhibition the map of Europe underwent a drastic and unexpected change. The fall of communist regimes in Eastern Europe bore witness to Czechoslovakia's "Velvet Divorce," the bloody fragmentation of Yugoslavia and, perhaps most surprising of all, the disintegration of the mighty Soviet Union itself. In its place stood over a dozen new countries, most of which I'd never hear of before.

As a new philatelist this new order was all very exciting, for my youthful naivety failed to comprehend the terrible social upheaval these countries were undergoing. Stamps started appearing bearing unfamiliar names for the very first time, while others inscribed "Eesti", "Latvija" and "Lietuva"—Estonia, Latvia, and Lithuania in their native tongues—hadn't been seen for well over fifty years.

It was this event that sparked a life-long interest in the former USSR. This colossal nation, which had appeared to be so monolithic and indivisible, so impregnable and unyielding, turned out to be nothing of the sort. Russia and the Soviet Union had always appeared synonymous but it was in fact an incredibly diverse land that would be torn apart by the forces of ethnic nationalism, the fall of Communism akin to a house of cards crashing down.

Today it's hard to comprehend just how big the Soviet Union really was. Weighing in at over eight and a half million square miles, it covered an area roughly equivalent to the entire North American continent and was by far the largest modern nation state the world has ever seen. Its borders stretched for some thirty-seven thousand miles, from Scandinavia down through Eastern Europe and into Asia before looping back into the Arctic. It spanned eleven time zones and contained a huge diversity of landscapes and peoples. It was inconceivably gigantic.

I first visited what had once been Soviet territory in 2008. At the time I'd moved to the northern English city of Leeds not long before and I felt a long way both literally and metaphorically from my parents, both of whom had re-married and moved on with their lives. In particular I felt the distance from my dad and wanted to do something that would bring us closer together, to find some way of bonding.

The opportunity came when he was doing some re-search at the National Media Museum in nearby Bradford. We met up for a pub lunch, and during the meal I pro-posed that we take a trip.

"Sounds interesting, son. Where were you thinking of?" he asked between mouthfuls of meaty lasagne.

"Um, Belarus."

"Bela*where*?"

"Belarus. It's part of the former Soviet Union. Borders Poland and Ukraine. Apparently it's more like the com-munist old days than Russia is. Lots of socialist realism and the like. I think you'd like it."

He nodded his approval and so, a few months later, we found ourselves in Belarus. It'd be fair to say that it's not a country that's received a great deal of positive press in the West; it was once infamously described by then US Secretary of State Condoleezza Rice as an "outpost of tyranny," and moustachioed President Alexander Lukashenko—similarly dubbed "Europe's last dictator"—has ruled without interruption since 1994. It's also the only European country to practice the death penalty and is consistently ranked bottom continent-wide for its lack of democratic freedom.

This was also to be a trip on a budget. Direct flights into Minsk were prohibitively expensive so we decided to take a budget flight to Lithuania instead, travel into Belarus by train, and then leave by the same method via Warsaw. It also meant we'd get to see three countries for the price of one.

Lithuania was an unexpected breath of fresh air. Fun and quirky, we explored capital Vilnius and second-city Kaunas and found a friendly country well off the tourist radar but making huge strides both economically and politically. Indeed, it was immediately obvious that the state was doing all it could to distance itself from its previous incarnation as a Soviet Socialist Republic. Nowhere was this more obvious than at the Museum of Genocide Victims in Vilnius; here the Soviet era was not only presented as an occupation of one country by another but also as a time when the Soviet authorities undertook a deliberate and systematic policy of ethnic extermination against the Lithuanian people.

The contrast with the presentation of history we found in neighbouring Belarus was stark. In Minsk the monumental Museum of the Great Patriotic War presented the conflict as a titanic battle of Soviet good versus Nazi evil, with the Communist period remembered with great fondness. Even the name given to this struggle is charged with layered meaning, for the Great Patriotic War only covers the period following Operation Barbarossa. To this day Russian War memorials are dated 1941 to 1945, tacitly suggesting the Nazi invasion to be the start of the war and ignoring Stalin's forays into eastern Poland and the Baltics in the two years previously. And although Belarus and Lithuania both declared their independence from the USSR at roughly the same time each chose, intentionally or otherwise, to remember their participation in the Soviet state in a diametrically opposed fashion. In Belarus—or so we were led to believe—the only ethnic cleansing that went on was committed by the Germans.

It was an impression that I couldn't shake off during the two weeks we were out East. Whilst Lithuania did its best to vilify its past Belarus did its best to celebrate it. Indeed, statues of Lenin and hammer and sickles were so prevalent in the latter it was almost as if the USSR's breakup had never actually happened in the first place. I desperately wanted to go back and find out why.

But this would be difficult. I'd never had a job that paid much more than minimum wage, and there was no escaping the fact that no matter how tight the budget travel always costs money. Quite simply I couldn't afford it, particularly after another round of full-time education had left me with a mountain of debt and no obvious means of ever clearing it. So I began to look for other means of procuring funds.

A bit of online research revealed that there were lots of organisations offering money in the form of bursaries and grants for independent travel. Many of these were for relatively small amounts, usually meant as a part contribution to an expedition, while others had exceedingly idiosyncratic selection criteria or were instead intended for specific studies. Only a precious few were open to more general suggestions, but what they all had in common was that they were and are extremely competitive. It's not unusual for some to receive thousands of applications every year.

So it became something of a clandestine hobby to apply for these bursaries whenever I had the opportunity. Usually these would be rather lengthy and only occasionally quick, but I met with little success. Sometimes I would get through an initial stage or make a shortlist, but invariably they would all come back to me with a letter along the lines of *We regret to inform you…* or variations thereof.

After going through a particularly dry spell I stumbled across a relatively obscure organisation by the name of the Peter Kirk Memorial Fund and its European Travel Scholarship. Admittedly I'd never heard of Peter Kirk but it transpired that he had been appointed leader of the first British team at the European Parliament by Prime Minister Ted Heath when the United Kingdom joined the European Community in 1973. In any case, it certainly sounded promising: a grant to conduct a research project anywhere in Europe for a period of eight weeks or thereabouts.

And so I suggested that I visit Estonia, Latvia and Lithuania to examine how these countries had changed and developed since independence. Would they bear any semblance to their Soviet past? Would I be able to tell that I was in what was once the USSR? It was, I felt, an interesting and straightforward brief. I wanted to find out whether any tangible Soviet legacy had been left behind, whether that be in the physical infrastructure or in the hearts and minds of the local people. Themes such as nostalgia, inter-community relations, politics, religion and the whole socio-economic spectrum would all come under the microscope. Yes, it was broad, but I was confident that my enthusiasm would translate into an interesting and stimulating project.

It was with a by-now familiar sense of frustration when I received a letter telling me that once again I'd been unsuccessful. The only consolation was that I'd thoroughly enjoyed the initial research that had gone into my submission and I decided there and then that this was something I had to do, grant or no grant. So I promptly turned my attention towards the next doomed application.

Yet it was not to be thus. Shortly afterwards I received a call to say that one of the successful candidates had withdrawn from the interview process, and would I be in a position to take their place? I booked my bus down to London that night.

The proposal was simple: I was to spend two months in the Baltics, starting in Estonia and generally working my way south through Latvia and into Lithuania. During this time I would seek out areas of life where the Soviet Union had left a tangible mark—and perhaps where it hadn't—and talk to anyone with a story to tell. It didn't matter if they had experienced life in the Soviet Union first-hand or were of the new generation born and raised after the dreams of a socialist utopia had been dashed by the irresistible forces of the market economy.

But it would be more than just a series of cosy chats over cups of coffee. I wanted to understand how the interpretation and reinterpretation of history can and does vary so dramatically over a short geographic space. True, this couldn't seriously be considered an in-depth piece of scientific research, but then that wasn't my intention; I wanted a personal exploration of the Baltic condition, for this to be a journey into the lives and stories that have shaped and reshaped this small corner of Europe. Fortunately for me, the trustees of the Peter Kirk Fund were convinced.

Of course the project presented an immediate problem: how would I, being resolutely monolingual, actually meet people in order to interview them? Sure, I could fire off a bunch of e-mails to university professors and local politicians, but I knew this wouldn't be an accurate representation of the view on the streets. I was also painfully aware that as generous as the grant was, when broken down on a day-by-day basis I was going to struggle to cover all my expenses. Little did I realise that the solution to both problems lay in the same place: by sleeping at strangers' houses.

It was an idea my friend Tom suggested one evening during a bout of aimless late-night television watching. I'd known him a long time; we'd been at school together and despite going our separate ways at university we had by coincidence both ended up in Yorkshire. Being conspicuously southern probably encouraged both of us to hang out together, in a sort of state of mutual solidarity.

Now apparently a friend of a friend of Tom's had travelled throughout a swathe of South America and had paid next to nothing for accommodation by "couchsurfing," which basically meant sleeping for free on sofas and spare beds offered by likeminded individuals. Quite frankly it sounded absurd but it was worthy of investigation, so despite my reservations I had a look online to see what was out there.

Well, it turned out that couchsurfing is quite a big thing. Whole networks exist of individuals who advertise any sort of spare sleeping space that they have at home—a sofa, bed, floor and so on—and let travellers crash there for free. Mostly it's for similar reasons: many hosts have done the same themselves on their travels and want to give something back, whereas others simply love meeting new people from all over the world. It all sounded wonderfully altruistic.

I was intrigued. I sent off a load of requests to individuals in Finland and Estonia, my first ports of call. Most of them didn't reply, and those who did mostly said they weren't going to be around or were otherwise unavailable. But one kind woman from Tartu soon explained the likely reason why I was finding it so difficult: I had no references.

Out of necessity couch surfing places a great deal of emphasis on trust which, when you come to think of it, is probably just as well. Hosts need to feel safe with the person staying with them; likewise "surfers" need to feel comfortable in a stranger's home and both need reassurance that the other is not a crazed axe murderer. The way couchsurfing websites usually resolve this problem is to use a system of feedback not unlike that used by the likes of numerous auction and travel websites. After a stay both parties rate their experience and these reviews are made publically available, thereby enabling future hosts and surfers to make informed decisions on whether or not they wish to meet the other person—the idea being that someone with lots of positive references is less likely to be trouble than someone with none. Without references I was essentially an unknown quantity and therefore in couchsurfing's world virtually unhostable.

Undeterred I tried again, this time explaining the project and the reason for my visit to the Baltics in full.

It seemed to work: I bagged places to stay in Helsinki, Tallinn and Tartu, and I felt sure that more would follow when I was on the road. The name of my soon-to-be-host in Tallinn was Mari.

CHAPTER 3

Swimming Nuns

* * *

Sofia perched on the sofa in Mari's apartment, cup in hand. She smiled as she recounted our meeting in the restaurant earlier that day, and then asked me what it was that brought me to Estonia. I told her about the project.

"Well it's interesting you mention it, because it's an issue that affects my own family," she said. "My grandparents are—what's the word?—'aliens,' because they cannot pass the citizenship tests."

"It's true" blurted Mari as she dashed past, hair straighteners in hand. "She's a Russian!" Sofia stuck out her tongue in response.

I was intrigued. "So what does it mean for your grandparents, then? Are they resentful? Does it annoy you?"

"Well, it means they can't vote and they can't travel to the rest of the EU as easily as we can. But they have some family in Saint Petersburg and they can go there without a visa. I would need one if I went. So it could be worse, I guess."

Sofia was a language student at the nearby University of Tallinn and had excellent English. I was curious to know if there were any tensions between young Estonians and Russians, but she told me that for young people this wasn't really the case. She and Mari were, she said, a good example of this in action.

"So do Estonians and Russians live apart? Are they segregated?"

"Sometimes they are, I guess. I don't really know; I speak Estonian and have lots of Estonian friends, so I've never really thought about it."

"But I guess that isn't the same for your grandparents?"

"No, I suppose not. But I think as aliens get older they will get smaller as a group because young Russian-speakers, well we are speaking Estonian all the time."

The segregation issue was one that I found particularly interesting. I'd done part of my degree in Belfast, and right across Northern Ireland areas of predominantly Catholic and Protestant people continue to be divided by "peace-lines," the euphemistic name for the numerous barriers that keep the warring communities apart. It would appear that despite the tensions no such physical walls existed in Estonia, but I did wonder whether it might be true in a more existential sense. However such thoughts would have to wait, for Mari reappeared, ready to party Tallinn-style. Before long we had disappeared deep into the night.

The next morning I trudged from the apartment into town. The roads were clogged with rush-hour traffic as people hurried to work, but despite this Baltic gridlock the northern air was cool, crisp and refreshing. Tallinn is so far north that it's on a similar latitude to the Orkney Islands, and had I been able to whistle I almost certainly would have done so; the dull ache at the back of my head couldn't dampen my spirits.

Ah, last night. We'd all gone into town and visited a few of Tallinn's bars. Some were new, some were old, some catered almost exclusively to the burgeoning trade in stag parties—this constitutes the stereotypical view of British tourists, or so I was told. Some of the more interesting were reserved for locals and we ended up in one of these, a strange but hip little venue that felt like it had been built in what had once been someone's home without them even bothering to remove the furniture and furnishings. The house speciality was an unusual but pleasant mixture of vodka and coffee, served as a warm shot. It turned out they went down rather too well.

I was heading towards the Museum of Occupations, on the corner of Toompea and Kaarli puiestee. Located just outside the walls of the Old Town, I found it down a leafy street not far from the hill that once constituted the political heart of medieval Tallinn.

Unlike the majority of the Tallinn I'd seen so far the museum was situated in a modern building. A concrete-and-glass structure had been slightly raised at ground level, providing an opening into a small courtyard filled with birch trees. A solid-looking metal door inscribed Okupatsioonide Muuseum in strong capital letters marked the entrance to the museum proper.

Only a couple of other visitors were there. I bought my ticket at a little desk, where the smiling attendant proceeded to tell me about the museum and what I could expect to see. "Please, do ask questions if you need answer," she said sweetly.

Inside, the museum had exhibits relating to both the Nazi and Soviet periods; a pair of stylised trains dominated the main room, adorned with a swastika and hammer and sickle respectively. All around the edge of the museum I could see battered old brown suitcases, each of which represented one of the innumerable Estonians deported before, during and after World War II.

The museum also featured plenty of paraphernalia from those dark times: propaganda posters, military uniforms, surveillance equipment and so on. There was the tiny cell with barely enough room to stand, where individuals would sometimes be kept for hours or days at a time, and a section of wall with an almost invisible spy-hole used for the clandestine monitoring of suspects. In the basement was an assortment of Soviet statuary, including a huge marble Lenin head that was slowly gathering dust.

At the back of the museum there was a series of videos of contemporary newsreel footage where attention was noticeably heavier on the USSR. Indeed, it felt like the videos were essentially glossing over the four-year German occupation during World War II: no mention of the Estonian Legion (a home-grown unit that served with the Waffen

SS) or of the frequent collaboration between locals and occupiers. Were the Nazis not also occupiers?

It set me wondering. Perhaps this asymmetric focus
was because the Soviet period had been so traumatic and so
devastating, or simply that it was much longer in duration
than the German occupation. Or, given that at the outset
of World War II Estonia had only won its independence
from Russia two decades before, maybe the Soviets were
seen as the greater threat to freedom and any cooperation
with German forces was merely the result of political and
military pragmatism—as had happened with Finland and
its wartime Axis alliance. Or perhaps, as Valeria had suggested earlier, it was about narratives. Any suggestion of
wartime collaboration with the Nazis would not sit easily
with a national narrative of an Estonian David ultimately
defeating the Soviet Goliath. It was hard to tell.

I meandered away from the museum and past the
leafy Hirvepark, scene of an anti-Soviet demonstration in
1987 marking the anniversary of the Molotov-Ribbentrop
Pact, not far from the fine medieval Kiek-in-de-Kök
tower. Nearby was Vabaduse Väljak, a square once used
for parades on Soviet holidays but now dominated by the
Freedom Monument, an Estonian cross mounted on a pil-
lar of frosted glass. It was apparently made to resemble ice,
representing freedom's fragility. Strictly speaking it was
not anti-Soviet because in this case "freedom" alluded to
the anti-Russian independence struggles of 1918 to 1920,
but its unashamed patriotism and potential relevance to

any contemporary confrontation with Russia couldn't be denied. I took a few pictures before heading back into the city's historical charms.

I made my way up to Toompea, the limestone outcrop that stands tall over the rest of the city. Once the site of a castle, this was the religious and political nerve centre of medieval Tallinn; it now plays host to a number of state institutions and the like. It also has two of Tallinn's most beautiful churches, the squat Orthodox Alexander Nevsky Cathedral and the Lutheran Toomkirik.

The hill was a little quieter than the city below, and from the top it offered splendid views across the Old Town and beyond. The strategic value of Toompea and of Tallinn was readily apparent; wedged between the sea to the north and Lake Ülemiste to the south, it was in prime position to dominate this part of the Gulf of Finland. This was as true in the Soviet era as it was in medieval times; for all its gargantuan bulk the USSR had comparatively little access to unfrozen seas, rendering almost the entire Baltic coast a sensitive area: the Soviet Union's window onto the West.

Suitably enough the town, it seems, was once a hotbed of le Carré–style Cold War espionage. I could see across to the Viru Hotel, where a secret floor has been recreated to depict its former life as a KGB surveillance centre. Complete with telephones and other bits of surveillance apparatus, officers would spend their days intercepting radio signals from Helsinki and passing messages on to

Moscow. Predictably, almost the entire hotel was once bugged.

Slightly closer stood the mighty spire of St. Olaf's Church, once the world's tallest building and still the highest structure in Tallinn. This too had once been appropriated by the Soviets, who used it as a radio and television-jamming station. It's now a Baptist church and a popular tourist viewing point.

As I gazed out over the sea I tried to imagine this city as it might have been thirty or forty years ago, a time remembered with anger and bitterness by many and yet one that was now successfully promoted to curious tourists in their thousands. I realised that this contradiction was going to take some time to understand.

One place where these two Tallinns meet is Patarei Merekindlus. I found this decaying edifice near the harbour, hidden away from the centre of town. At first I thought it was closed, since a heavy padlocked gate created the impression that the place was deserted and off-limits. Further investigation, however, revealed that the main entrance was confusingly not on the street that bears the prison's name but was in fact a short distance away, around the corner.

I walked in, past a watchtower slowly rusting in the salty sea air and along the sides of the forbidding prison's exterior, where thick metal bars covered each of the windows and which were themselves set in solid white-washed walls some three storeys high. The path took me down to a small hut, where an elderly lady sold me a ticket and guidebook for a few euros. A middle-aged man—I assumed he also worked at the site—lounged nearby, and as I reappeared from the hut into the bright sunshine he nodded in my direction and asked "English?" I affirmed, and he proceeded to give me a few directions about the place. "Go in please through there, that is the entrance. You can move around the buildings this is okay. And please, if you turn right and through the door"—here he paused ever-so-slightly, a hint of a smile playing on his lips—"there is room for executions. Enjoy please."

I couldn't help dwelling on this curious turn of phrase as I entered the central courtyard, a wedge shape surrounded on all three sides by the triangular walls of the prison proper. I turned right as the man suggested, through a doorway and into a dingy corridor that was noticeably cooler than outside. A cold dankness hung in the air.

After a short distance I emerged into a room that somehow seemed even grimier than those I'd just walked through. Yellow and white paint was peeling from cold hard walls and a weak light filtered in through a small grilled window, casting a murky shadow across the floor. But my attention was drawn to what was standing in the centre of the room: a dirty wooden ladder leading up to a rusty hook in the wall, a square hole in the ground just in front of it. The drop, for hanging prisoners. All that was missing was the rope.

In the deathly-still room you could have heard a pin drop. The atmosphere was damp and oppressive, and I couldn't bear to stand in there for more than a couple of minutes; the thought that so many souls had ended their last days in this darkest of places was so palpable it made me shudder. To get back into the outside air of the courtyard was blessed relief.

The rest of the prison had been left to rot, with many of the original furnishings left intact. According to the guidebook the facility, once a Tsarist-era naval fort, had been in use to incarcerate inmates from 1920 to as recently as 2002. Hundreds had been executed there, the book went on, with the killing reaching its apogee during the Soviet period; indeed so many had perished that one room had been painted a deep red to hide the blood spilled from the gunshots. Small holes still peppered the walls.

I travelled freely through the still-deserted prison. In the courtyard were tiny exercise yards with barely enough room to take more than a couple of paces; above ran a walkway so that prisoners couldn't escape the guards' ever-watchful eye. Nearby stood a large apple tree, said to have been planted by the last pre-war prison chief.

The cells were even grimmer. Much of the contents had been left intact—bedframes, mattresses, damaged books and so on. Magazine pages full of colourful images of film stars and cars had been pasted all over the wall like a window on the world for the inmates, a way of escaping the crushing reality of prison life. In the library books (mostly in Russian) were gathering dust on the shelves, where they had probably lain untouched for years; perhaps creepiest of all was the medical wing, with its glass cabinets and discarded equipment.

A more thoroughly depressing place would have been hard to imagine. It was time to move on.

The queue in the railway station was progressing at an agonisingly slow pace. I nervously glanced at my watch: four minutes until the train would depart. Why was it, I thought, that some people take forever to buy tickets and why do they always insist on doing so when I'm in a hurry? What on earth is taking them so long?

Finally, I got to the booth.

"A ticket to Tartu, please," I blurted out.

"Oh, you don't buy that here. You must get it on the train," said the stony-faced ticket attendant drily, as if it were the stupidest thing she'd heard all day.

I desperately wanted to ask why it said "Tallinn-Tartu" next to the counter that specifically advertised the sale of train tickets but given the circumstances I thought better of it. I dashed outside to where Mari was guarding her bicycle and she slapped her hand to her forehead when I informed her of the situation. "Of course! I completely forgot that you can buy tickets on the train!"

We hugged, and I said that I would be returning to Tallinn soon. Mari smiled. "I know. Let me know when you're back. Have a nice time in Tartu."

And with the red flash of her coat she was gone.

I ran to the train only seconds before its doors slid shut. It was busy, and instead of taking a seat I decided to stand in the compartment at the end of the carriage so I could fully enjoy the view from the window. It was a lovely sunny day, with azure blue skies all the way to the horizon.

The journey to Tartu took just over a couple of hours, passing through a largely flat and bucolic landscape of farmland, forests and swamps, all staples of the Estonian countryside. Every now and then the train would pull to a halt at a small station in the middle of nowhere, and a few people would get on and off. At one point a group of young soldiers dressed in fatigues got on board and took their seats where they could, the unfortunate one or two having to stand.

Tartu is Estonia's second city and is the country's intellectual heart, a sort of Baltic Oxford or Cambridge if you will. The 370-year-old university is the most prestigious seat of learning in the region and something like a fifth of the city's population of 100,000 are students, at least during term time. It's also very "Estonian"; migration from other parts of the Soviet Union was relatively low and today a smaller proportion of the inhabitants count Russian as their first language compared to most other urban settlements in Estonia.

The university was also the primary reason for my trip to the city. I'd arranged to meet a few academics and students from the Centre for Baltic Studies, who had been particularly interested in the project and were keen to help.

I'd also reconfirmed my couchsurfing host, this time with the woman who had originally told me all about the referencing system when I was first making enquiries back in England. I met Margit at the station, and as we walked the short distance to her flat we spoke more about the purpose of my visit and life in Tartu in general. "You've picked a good time to be here," she said. "Right now it's the Student Days, so there's a lot of parties going on with all the different fraternities. And it's also Walpurgis Night; do you have this celebration in England? There will be fireworks and music, we can go tonight if you like."

We turned down Kastani street—the name means "chestnut," which pleased me—and shortly arrived at Margit's home, a pretty green wooden building divided into a couple of apartments. We entered the bottom flat and were greeted by a large and extremely friendly orange tomcat. "He's called Zeppelin," explained Margit, giving him a rub on the head, "because of his size."

I dumped my things and we set off for the centre of town. The bright sunshine had continued into the evening, bathing the streets in a warm ethereal glow which invited a calm and unhurried pace. As we strolled down Vanemuise Margit told me about her life. Only a couple of months older than me, she had been born and raised in Tartu and was currently working for a government-funded organisation that coordinated international research projects. She seemed proud of her city, and it wasn't difficult to see why: first impressions were favourable, of a leafy and tidy place unscarred by unsightly brutalist construction. She had long dark hair, wore glasses, and had a soft-spoken manner that hid a keenly sharp intellect.

We emerged into Raekoja plats, Tartu's modest but very enticing central square. In the centre was a quaint fountain topped with a statue of a youthful couple kissing underneath an umbrella that had become something of a symbol of the city. I could also feel an excitable tension in the air; the cafés and bars were fit to burst and the square's cobbled surface was thronging with students, some dressed in formal evening wear with student caps that looked a bit like squashed fezzes. "They're part of the fraternities," Margit explained. Most of them were Estonian, but I thought I could hear smatterings of German, Lithuanian and Russian too.

We grabbed a bite to eat before heading down to the river, the slow-moving Emajõgi. It was dark by now, and as we pushed our way through the crowds to secure a good spot we could see a large installation of some kind lit up on a small footbridge and hovering a few feet above the water's surface. A bare-chested man began to play a steady drumbeat before being joined by an unseen woman chanting in Estonian—a traditional type of singing that Margit said was known as *regilaul*. It was hauntingly beautiful, and the multitudes fell silent in what felt like a unified act of reverential respect.

Singing has had a special place in Estonian cultural life for decades, even playing a key part in the independence movement during the 1980s. Special outdoor arenas known as "song grounds" would host huge events, where thousands would converge to wave flags and sing popular patriotic anthems. In September of 1988 a gathering of some 250,000 Estonians—out of a national population of 1.5 million at the time—converged in Tallinn, which led commentators to dub the Estonian push for independence the "Singing Revolution."

After the regilaul came more drummers, this time with sparks flying from their instruments, and colourful fireworks and the lighting of small flames on little barges in the river. It was a peculiar mixture of sombreness and celebration, of Nordic tradition, of a paganesque affinity with nature and a tangible sense of pride in national identity.

As we returned to Margit's flat she asked if I had brought anything smart to wear. "Because I am going to one of the fraternities tonight. It will be fun, lots of drinking and partying. Very much a Tartu tradition." I looked down at my scruffy jeans and trainers and sadly shook my head.

Margit got back in at four in the morning. I didn't even stir.

Eneli was already waiting for me when I arrived at Tartu's Café Pierre, a trendy establishment in Raekoja plats. She was reading a book on Basque culture, and as I was about to introduce myself her friend Oskar arrived. Both were students at the university, and they were more than happy to talk to me about their understanding of Estonia's Soviet history. They were native Estonian speakers and had typically Nordic looks; Eneli with a slight build, Oskar tall and both blond. I ordered a drink, and we sat and talked in the bright morning sunshine about their hopes and fears for the future.

"I think there are two kinds of people in Estonia," said Oskar. "There are the rich, and then there are the poor. I think the gap is perhaps worse now than it was when our parents were young."

"So do you think that can lead to some nostalgia for Soviet times?" I asked.

"Perhaps. We hear stories from our parents and they're the most influential source of our opinions, I would say. But with nostalgia there is also sadness, because yes some things were better, but there was also oppression, and this affected everyone. Estonians, Russians, all of us."

"True, but there were still divisions between Estonians and Russians during the Soviet occupation," interrupted Eneli. "There has always been this mutual suspicion. Russians like to remind us of Soviet times, especially because they do not think of those times as an occupation, and this will always be the case I think."

"So could this perhaps cause trouble in the future, perhaps another Bronze Night?"

"Absolutely, of course. We are always worried that this can happen again."

Eneli looked at me earnestly with her blue eyes. "We are scared of Russia. We are scared that Russia will come across our border again, just like they did in the war. Putin looks to Estonia and sees all these Russians here. Just look at what happened in Georgia, or Ukraine. Anywhere with Russian people will not be safe."

I wondered if she thought that Estonia's membership of the European Union and NATO made her feel more secure.

"Maybe a little. There is some collective security for us, which the Baltic region needs. We have always worked well with Latvia and Lithuania economically and defensively. But we are small, and because of our Soviet history the West thinks of us as Eastern Europe, when in fact we are part of the North—like Scandinavia."

Indeed Estonia, Latvia and Lithuania signed a trilateral agreement to bolster their collective defences several years prior to joining NATO, and I would have been surprised if Russia thought itself confident enough to violate the territorial integrity of a member of a nuclear alliance even if it had openly seethed at the sight of countries once firmly in its orbit joining up. After all, does Article 5 of the NATO treaty not state that an attack on one member state is an attack on all? Still, a potent combination of Russian nationalism, irredentism, the desire of Moscow to "protect its citizens abroad," and the fear of isolation by its one-time Cold War foes was clearly enough to make at least some people who live close to Russia's borders watch nervously over their shoulders.

When I asked them if they would ever consider emigrating they shook their heads. "No," said Oskar, "our place is here. Maybe we might work for a year or two abroad, but we will want to return to Estonia." I wasn't sure if this was more patriotism or pragmatism at work, but I didn't doubt his sincerity.

As they said their goodbyes, I bought another drink and typed up some notes. The day before Margit had suggested we visit her parents, who lived a mile or two away in another part of town. The short walk had taken us through a pleasant part of the city, with tidy wooden buildings from the Tsarist and "first-independence" eras lining the streets. At one point a panorama opened up, and in the distance grey monolithic Soviet apartment blocks that would become such a frequent sight on the journey lined the horizon. "Most Russians in Tartu live there," said Margit, referring to the descendants of the workers who came here in times past from all corners of the USSR. It's more than likely that these were *Khrushchyovka* or *Khrushcheby* (a portmanteau of Khrushchev and *trushcheby*, the Russian word for slum): cheap prefabricated apartment blocks constructed in the 1960s to ease the intense overcrowding in towns and cities across the Soviet Union.

When we reached their home Margit's mother and father were both out in the garden, making the most of the morning sunshine. Kersti and Jaan were a middle-aged couple, ethnic Estonians who readily seized on the opportunity of having a couple of extra pairs of hands by pressing us into service with promises of homemade fruit juice and snacks as encouragement. So it was that we found ourselves clearing away dead leaves from the strawberry patch.

It was a decent-size allotment; aside from strawberries they also grew cabbages, carrots, and an assortment of other vegetables. I could see that other gardens nearby were also well-stocked, a testament to the fertile soil and sense of self-reliance in these parts.

By the time we'd filled up a bag with the literal fruit of our endeavours Kersti had brought out the refreshments, and we gratefully sat and helped ourselves to warm meat-filled pastries and the tastiest blackberry juice I could ever remember drinking. Between stuffed mouthfuls I asked my hosts about their lives in Tartu.

Kersti was a friendly woman with glasses and a warm smile who had previously worked in local government but had taken early retirement on health grounds. Could she ever have imagined an independent Estonia back in Soviet times? No, she said, no one even entertained it as a possibility. She, like so many other Estonians of her generation, had joined the Communist Party, but this wasn't so much for ideological reasons as simply doing what was expected of them; in many ways it was key to professional advancement. Curiously it also transpired that she'd been to Leeds as part of a healthcare delegation about a decade earlier.

Jaan nodded throughout, but I wasn't sure how much he understood of what was being said; he spoke no English—not unusual for those who received their education in Soviet times—and when he did speak Margit was on hand to translate. Jaan had also been a member of the Communist Party and was a refrigeration engineer, working on Soviet ships before Estonia's independence. His job saw him travel all over Europe, and this made me especially curious.

"What was it like working on the ships?" I asked. Estonia had been regarded as something of a centre of maritime industry in the USSR; indeed, Tallinn proudly hosted the sailing events during the 1980 Moscow Olympics.

"It was hard work," he said, "but I enjoyed it. For those times it was well-paid, and I preferred working on the boat to being stuck in a factory somewhere." He chuckled as he remembered, his bushy white moustache tracing the outline of his mouth.

"And there was a mixture of people on the ships, from all over the Soviet Union. I worked with Russians, with Tartars and Kalmyks, too."

I asked him if their movements had been restricted when they were docked in foreign ports.

"Oh yes, of course we were allowed on shore, but we could only go in groups and never on our own. This was to stop us from defecting, you see."

Had he ever been to the UK?

"Aberdeen!" he beamed. There was no need to translate.

I topped up my glass of juice. Kersti picked up the black-and-white cat that had been brushing by her feet and gave it a warm hug. I wondered out loud, were things better now?

They all nodded. "I think overall things are better," said Kersti. "Before we couldn't travel, and we were told that the West was a bad place; now I can go there and see that it isn't. But," she said after a pause, "there is probably more uncertainty. Back then, you could always get a job, and people had more security. It's possible that it's not like that anymore."

It was a lament that I was to hear more than once throughout the journey.

After we bid our farewells Margit and I headed into town, both feeling good about our morning's work. Down by the river further festivities were taking place, with students in fancy dress lining up to compete in a wacky boat race. We took our places among the crowd by the river's edge, cheering on the homemade boats as they made their way around a circular course. I particularly liked the Teletubbies and the zombie nuns.

I mentioned to Margit her parents' views on the stability of Soviet life, and she nodded. "Yes," she said, "a lot of older people have these opinions. It's very common."

"So can there be conflicts between older and younger people when it comes to the past?"

"Yes, definitely. Very often the older people can be annoyed when they see younger generations treating the past in a trivial way. Sometimes the students will have pretend-communist parties where they dress up in uniforms and get really drunk. They see it as disrespectful, I think."

A cheer went up from the crowd as one of the nuns fell habit-first into the water.

It was another fine morning as I made my way up the hill to the university. The social sciences department was located in Tartu's former maternity hospital—Margit joked that virtually the whole town, including her, had been born there—and I easily found the big yellow building past the Angel's Bridge, a neat nineteenth-century construction that was recovering from a recent arson attack.

The day had not started well. Before arriving in Estonia I was told that the interviews I'd arranged via the university would be postponed by a few days because of the student celebrations, and of those I'd been particularly pleased to secure a meeting with a woman named Marju Lauristin. Marju had played a prominent part in Estonia's independence movement in the late 1980s, cofounding Rahvarinne ("Popular Front") and serving as a government minister in the period immediately following secession from the Soviet Union. Today she served mainly as a well-respected political pundit and university professor, and my gaining an audience with her was something of a coup.

As instructed, I rang her in the morning of what I assumed was the rearranged day to arrange the time for our interview. "Hello. I was expecting you three days ago," came the flat reply. "Today I am going to Riga and I won't be back for a while. Maybe you could contact me again when you are next in Tartu. Goodbye." I felt like crying.

But all was not lost. I strolled into the reception area, where I found a lady sitting behind a neat desk reading a book. Adopting what I assumed to be my most apologetic look, I asked her the way to the social sciences department.

A raised eyebrow looked up from the book and eyed me slowly up and down. Then she shrugged. I tried another tack.

"Hi, do you know the way to Andu Rammer's office? Andu Rammer?"

Again, I was met with an uninterested shrug that seemed to me to be bordering almost on contempt. I indicated as best I could that perhaps she could allow me to try and find the office myself. The woman waved me away in irritation with barely a second glace and simply carried on reading.

After what felt like an eternity I eventually found Andu's office on the top floor; despite arriving at reception in good time I was several minutes late after running up and down pretty much every corridor in the entire building. He laughed when I explained why I'd had difficulty finding him: "That receptionist has never spoken to me, either."

Andu was a sociology lecturer, and he started by running through a potted history of Estonia from the Second World War to the present. Much of this was already familiar to me, and he agreed when I suggested that history had become a very charged and controversial topic within Estonia.

"But it does explain," he went on, "why there is so much insecurity within the country, and why Estonians fear their Russian neighbours." For many Estonians, it would seem, Russian speakers are a potential "fifth column" and Russia is still very much a threat to their national sovereignty. And it wasn't just war that Estonians feared: it was the idea that a Russophile cultural creep that threatened to drown out a nation of barely a million indigenous souls was a very distinct possibility. I realised that these were similar sentiments to those that Eneli and Maarja had expressed just a short while before.

I asked Andu about "alien citizens," a policy which, if implemented in other parts of Europe, would likely have caused a public uproar. "Yes, I can see why others would find this difficult to understand. But there are benefits, of course. Aliens can visit Russia visa-free."

I had two more meetings that day in the former maternity hospital. Heiko Pääbo and Dagmar Kutsar both offered related interpretations of the Estonian-Russian cultural conflict; Heiko spoke of such concepts as "national narratives" and "collective memory," while Dagmar suggested that national myths are created in times of uncertainty. It was as if the Soviet period had induced a collective sense of post-traumatic stress, where Russians were (and still are) automatically equated with the idea of national suppression.

These were interesting if slightly academic concepts, and as I sat on a bench shortly afterwards eating cheese sandwiches within the grounds of the city's ruined cathedral I tried to take stock of the direction the study was going in. I had originally foreseen myself spending the bulk of my time gawping at an array of statues and Soviet iconography and the like, much like I'd done in Belarus, and yet here I was tackling high-level ideas of cultural division and ethnic conflict. Could it be that the Soviet legacy was found not in infrastructure or the arts but rather in the people who are left behind?

That afternoon I went for a run around Tartu. From Margit's place on Kastani I headed towards the centre of town, past the building on Vanemuise where the Treaty of Tartu (in which the Bolshevik government recognised Estonian independence and renounced all claims to the region in perpetuity) was signed in 1920. A little further and I reached the Emajõgi and the bridge where I'd heard that haunting regilaul a couple of nights before. The sun was still shining brightly, and as I made my way along the riverbank I passed a couple of rowers sculling across the gleaming waters. Before long I reached a small sandy beach and couldn't help but stop for a while; the trees on the opposite bank were cast in perfect reflection in a scene of complete tranquillity. The only sound was an occasional "plop," coming from a nearby collection of reeds. Closer inspection proved this to be caused by a small family of frogs.

I set off again, beginning the long loop back to Raekoja plats and the university that took me past Tartu's song grounds where regular festivals attract singers from all over Estonia; Margit would later show me some clips online in which hundreds of singers would gather and sing in unison. She even recognised some of the faces in the crowds. Beyond the grounds was a ramshackle but handsome neighbourhood of streets known collectively as Supilinn—"Soup Town"—so named because the dusty streets were named after vegetables, like Herne ("pea") and Meloni ("melon").

By the time I got back to Kastani I must have looked a sorry state, dripping with sweat and feeling desperately unfit. Before I'd started the trip I'd promised myself that I would try to keep in shape, coming up with an ambitious fitness regimen to stick to which in the main largely consisted of running. I even brought a T-shirt and shorts just for the purpose.

It was the only time I used them.

The KGB Cells Museum is housed in the ominous-sounding Hallis majas (the "Grey House") on the corner of Riia and Pepleri. This was the former site of the regional headquarters of the Soviet secret police; in the basement, the tiny cramped chambers in which political prisoners would be interned before being exiled to Siberia and worse are maintained in their original state.

It took me a little while to find the entrance. When I did eventually find it I was led down some stairs into the building's basement and into a small reception area, where a young man sat behind a counter reading a book with a picture of Lenin on the cover. I handed over the entrance fee, mumbled my thanks, and set off to have a look around.

Some of the cells had been fitted out with displays dedicated to the people who had passed through its grim walls during the mass deportations of 1941 and 1949. Most of the accompanying text was in Estonian only, but this didn't matter: grainy photos of exiles eking out a living in the frozen wastes of Siberia, as well as original clothing and handicrafts from the gulags, served to provide a compelling history of the ultimately futile resistance to Soviet rule. Some of these were members of underground patriotic groups, such as the local "Blue-Black-and-White" (the colours of the Estonian flag), which mainly attracted teenagers. Many were to be subsequently deported.

The other rooms had been recreated to look as they would have done when they were in use. The cells were dark, damp and dingy, and each had a heavy metal door; in one a picture of Stalin on the wall surveyed a rudimentary office replete with desk and chair, whilst others were simply empty. The atmosphere was deeply oppressive, and it was hard to shake off the feeling that this was a place that had witnessed many unhappy memories. To me it seemed to offer a more genuinely discomforting account of the Soviet period compared to the Museum of Occupations, perhaps because it spoke of events that occurred *in situ*; the feeling I got was not dissimilar to that of Patarei.

After a while it was time to leave, and I dutifully trekked back to Margit's. She had already gone to work earlier that morning and had left me the key to her flat so that I could pick up my gear. I gave Zeppelin the cat one final rub, left a bottle of wine on the table, and locked the door behind me. I had a train to catch.

CHAPTER 4

The Gunman

∗ ∗ ∗

I'D GONE BACK TO TALLINN. Mari's prediction had been
entirely accurate; I felt like I'd had several productive days'
work in Tartu and I wanted a bit of time out to take stock
of what I'd learned, or at least that's what I was telling myself. Truth is, I wanted to see Mari again.

I found her, as before, at the restaurant. It was busy, I
mean really busy; I spied her rushing around and mouthed
a silent "hi" before taking the last available table and or-
dering some food. I found a nice little spot in a corner out
of the way, and typed up some notes from the previous few
days. Before long a steaming hot pile of curry and rice appeared in front of me.

As I tucked in the strains of faux-Eastern music that
had been playing gently over the speakers suddenly dipped,
to be replaced by a new, louder drumbeat. From behind
an arch a belly dancer shimmied into view, replete with
flimsy costume, sparkling jewelled charms and bare mid-
riff, thrusting and shaking her way around the restaurant

tables. Perhaps it was my English reserve, but at first I felt slightly uncomfortable, embarrassed even. But as I looked around I could see the other diners smiling and clapping, the children wanting to take part.

"She's good," said Mari, who had joined me as I watched. I felt inclined to agree.

"I'm working late tonight," she went on, "and you probably won't want to be hanging around here all the time." She produced a key from her pocket and pressed it into my hand.

"Just go back to my apartment and I will meet you there later. You can remember where it is?"

It was evening, and my route towards Mari's home took me through some of the new Tallinn: shiny new shopping centres, cinemas and the obligatory McDonalds could be found scattered among gleaming towers of glass and steel. But dig a little deeper by going down some of the grimier side streets and you'll soon rediscover the Soviet Union in some of the older grey apartment buildings, slowly being pushed to the periphery by the inexorable march of Westernisation.

The brown-and-yellow block on Raua Street looked newer than its surroundings, but inside it was the same as the others: a new shell having simply been placed on an old Soviet heart. I climbed the musty stairs until I reached a heavy brown metal door. I put the key in the lock—one turn, two turns, three, *click*—before it opened into Mari's spacious flat.

I switched on the kettle and rustled up a cup of tea with some bags I'd found in a nearby supermarket. Stumbling across them had been an absolute godsend, for in its ultra-English *black-with-a-drop-of-milk-no-sugar-please* variety it's often not the easiest of beverages to source overseas—indeed, in much of Eastern Europe it's somewhat barbarically served with lemon, with nary a hint of dairy in sight. In truly stereotypical form I'm hopelessly addicted to the stuff, but in all the excitement and commotion of preparing for the big trip I'd somehow forgotten to pack any. So it was that even I couldn't begrudge the hefty price tag that its imported status demanded.

I powered up the laptop and did a bit of surfing, checking the news and the like in a rather aimless fashion. For some unfathomable reason I started watching a series of chat show clips, each more horrendous than the last. There was the one with the disputed paternity test, the one where a husband had cheated on a wife with a friend, the one with lots of swearing; and yet, like a car crash, it was hard to look away. I kept watching until the early hours of the morning.

I must have woken up at about eight, to another bright blue-skied morning; something of a theme it would seem, not that I was complaining. Outside the city was already alive with activity, with the streets slowly starting to fill with cars and pedestrians. Through the window I watched an elderly man walking a dog, which plodded along slowly beside him; it looked like a spaniel of some kind from where I was sitting, but it was hard to tell.

Inexplicably there was no sign of Mari; she hadn't come back from work and she wasn't replying to the text messages I'd sent shortly before drifting off to sleep the night before. This left me in a bit of a quandary; as far as I was aware I held the only key to the apartment, which meant that I couldn't very well leave without either leaving it unlocked or hoping that I bumped into her somewhere in Tallinn. Neither option sounded fool proof.

It did mean, however, that my involuntary incarceration was an opportunity to do a little homework. I decided that I'd leave the matter of the key until the afternoon and then make an executive decision, and until then I'd spend the time drinking more tea and working out where on earth I wanted to go next. My itinerary demanded that I be in Riga in time for the Victory Day celebrations on 9 May; other than that, the entire Baltic region was my metaphorical oyster.

I stared at the map in front of me. I could head west towards the coast where Estonia splinters into hundreds of islands as it greets the cold waters of the Baltic, or I could amble along the shore of the Gulf of Finland to Lahemaa, the very first national park in the Soviet Union and, according to my guidebook, home to Estonia's largest collection of "glacial erratics." These are large boulders that are conspicuously out of place in their surroundings, having been picked up and dumped elsewhere by glaciers and ice sheets back when Europe was a much colder place than it is today. In short, they're a geologist's dream.

Another route caught my eye: I could strike southwards towards the Latvian border and the shores of Lake Peipus, where a small community of Russian "Old Believers" still lives virtually undisturbed. These Orthodox Christians moved to the area in the eighteenth century to escape persecution from elsewhere in the Russian Empire; their name stems from the rejection of church reforms in the middle of the 1600s. While their numbers are thought to be in gradual decline, adherence to their own ways has largely prevented their assimilation with Russian migrants who came to Estonia after the Second World War and so remain very much a separate community. The area is also renowned for its charming wooden houses and churches.

But it was east that I was drawn. Here, right up against the border with Russia lies Estonia's third city, a place that is almost exclusively Russian-speaking and which sits on the river that bears its name—the Narva.

Narva in the 1930s was, by all accounts, a very attractive city indeed; contemporary travellers compared it favourably with Tallinn and it profited greatly from passing trade as a result of its location roughly halfway between the Estonian capital and Saint Petersburg. It was also the first real settlement in the region to undergo industrialisation, its mills transforming it into one of the largest centres of cotton manufacturing on the continent.

Of course, it was not to last. In the penultimate year of World War II almost the entire town was turned to dust by artillery as the front lines swept back into Estonia. A devastating aerial bombardment by the Soviet Air Force, combined with charges laid by the retreating Germans, took care of the rest.

At war's end the beautiful baroque old town was gone, replaced by a smouldering landscape of charred ruins. When the Soviet authorities decided to rebuild Narva anew they did so with the identikit apartment blocks that still stand to this day. This was a place I was clearly going to have to visit.

I checked the train times and saw that one was departing that evening; if I left soon I could make it. Yet I still hadn't heard from Mari; what the hell was I going to do with her key? And then, right on cue, I got a text message "Meet me at the railway station in an hour?" I hurriedly packed my things and rushed out the door, slamming it shut behind me.

When I arrived Mari was nowhere to be seen. I'd marched across the city with a heavy bag on my back at breakneck speed and I was hot and sweaty and not a little irritated. I hunted around the station inside and out, and eventually spied her on the street outside, hurrying towards me.

"Hey, I'm sorry I'm late!"

She was covered with the faint whiff of alcohol.

"That's okay. Um, where have you been?" I asked, only slightly suspiciously.

"Oh, well, when I working in the restaurant and then I got a message from a bar I sometimes work in asking if I could work so I said 'sure,' and then afterwards my friend asked me if I wanted to party at her place. So I went to hers and then was sleeping in the day."

All of which explained the radio silence pretty well. I rummaged in my pockets until I found the key and gave it to her.

"So," I asked, "what are you doing now?" I was wondering why she had asked to meet me at the station.

"Ah, I'm going home, to my parents' house in the country. My friend from school is having a party for her birthday—hey, do you want to come?"

I paused. During my time trapped in Mari's flat I'd managed to find a host in Narva who was willing to take me; it hadn't been easy because, unlike in Tallinn or Tartu, it appeared that few people there spoke English. Yet the thought of hanging out with Mari somewhere in rural Estonia was an opportunity that was too good to miss. The pause ended.

"Sure, that would be cool."

The train to Tapa was already waiting so we clambered on board, eschewing the Wi-Fi comforts of first class by pushing through to the back carriages. It was busy—Estonia's limited rail system only carries a few services a day—but we spied a couple of spare seats. Slumping herself against the window, Mari called her friend to let her know to expect an extra guest and I typed up a message to my contact in Narva to let him know that I wouldn't be coming that night.

Mari chatted away in Estonian, her grin betraying the fact that she was clearly looking forward to seeing the birthday girl. I looked out of the window, the turreted city walls soon giving way to slick modern office buildings. The scene was a familiar one, for the line to Tapa carries on to Tartu.

But then Mari's faced darkened, and as she finished her conversation she turned to me. It was bad news. "My friend, she says the party is only for family and close friends, because there is not much space and her family cannot speak English. I'm really sorry, I didn't think she would say this."

As I dwelled on this unexpected development and the missed connection to Narva Mari made a suggestion. "Right, I know what you can do. You can stay in my family's house whilst I go to the party; there's a computer you can use, and I promise I will not stay too late. You will be fine." She gave me a small, reassuring smile. I guess I didn't really have a choice.

Soon we pulled into Tapa's pleasing Tsarist-era train station. The town owes its existence to the railway; located at the junction of Estonia's two main lines, today it remains an important transit centre and training centre for the Estonian Defence Forces. Even the town's flag of three white lines on a red background is designed to evoke the rails that converge here.

We were early, so we went to a nearby supermarket to stock up on essentials: a chocolate bar, a few sweets and a couple of bottles of wine. "For the party," explained Mari.

Outside a battered car pulled up just as we were exiting the shop. The passenger door sprang opened, and a young man jumped out and gave Mari a hug before helping me put my bag in the boot and clambering back in. Mari and I got into the back and we set off at a blistering pace.

"This is my brother, and this"—pointing to the driver—"is my father." They both murmured a greeting as Mari repeated what she had just said in Estonian and I mumbled one back, holding on as we swept around a sharp corner. The car itself was full of junk that suggested one of the occupants was in the building trade; a few paint tins, some bits of wood and the like. There was that stale smell of alcohol in the air again, and as we once more emerged into the Estonian countryside I quickly realised that we were well and truly off the tourist track.

Mari had grown up in a little village called Ambla. Ambla was typical of many settlements in the area: small, provincial, remote, and distinctly down-at-heel. It had a church, some playing fields, and a smattering of the wooden houses of the sort I'd seen in Tartu and elsewhere. Mari's house was on the edge of the village, surrounded by attractive green meadows and pine trees.

The car pulled up and we all jumped out. It gave me a better opportunity to examine her dad, a white-haired man in what I judged to be his mid-fifties. He had piercing blue eyes, and as he looked me up and down I got the impression that life had not always been easy for him. Had it been the same for the rest of his family also, I wondered.

The bungalow in which I was to spend the night also looked like it had seen better days. It had a corrugated tin roof and end walls that appeared to be made of concrete breeze blocks topped with wood. The sides were blue, which gave the whole place a slightly disjointed and ramshackle feel. A dog, chained and tethered, barked at us in excitement.

The rest of Mari's family was waiting inside. Her mother beamed when we were introduced, shaking my hand warmly and ushering me towards a table and chairs in the central dining room before rushing to put the kettle on. There was also another woman, perhaps a few years younger than me, who turned out to be the girlfriend of Mari's brother and was the only other person in the house who spoke any English.

Perhaps the loveliest of them all, however, was Mari's niece, a sweet little girl of maybe five or six who was absolutely fascinated by this strange man who spoke a peculiar language and who smelled like he probably hadn't had a shower in a week. Later that afternoon Mari and I and the little girl had a competition to see who could jump the highest on the trampoline that was parked outside, and afterwards we fed apples to the horses who lived just across the road. All the time we were accompanied by the same infectious laugh.

"She cannot understand why you can't speak Estonian," whispered Mari as we sat in her old room, her childhood toys once again strewn around by young hands. I smiled at this, at the thought that language was no barrier to friendship at such a young age. She was drawing a picture with multi-coloured crayons, the whole time chatting in words I had no comprehension of but whose meaning I could deduce easily by the grins that conveyed them.

After we ate we discussed the plan for the evening. Mari and her mother would go to the party, which was taking place at her friend's house only a few hundred yards away, across a green pasture. Her brother would go elsewhere for the night, which would leave me with her father and her niece with the girlfriend. "It's okay," Mari assured me. "We won't be long. My dad will look after you."

So I sat myself down in the room with the television and had a browse through my guidebook. I lazily leafed through the pages, flicking to the back index to look under *T*. No mention of Tapa. According to the map the route from here to Narva looked to be a fairly straightforward one, with the nearby train offering a direct route to the Russian border.

I tried to imagine what the place where Estonia meets the largest country in the world would be like. Would there be barriers and watchtowers and armed guards with snap-happy Alsatian dogs? Would it be full of hi-tech gadgetry and CCTV cameras everywhere? Or would it be open, with only a cursory check of papers to impede one's way?

I've always found borders fascinating. There's just something a little magical about those long black lines on a map, whether they're made real by some great natural barrier like a river or a mountain chain, or from a linear pen stroke made with scant regard to physical reality. And there's always something intrinsically exciting about crossing that line; it propels us into a new culture, language, religion, or some other ethnological difference that is used to justify that other country's existence. For many of us crossing borders embodies one of the most exotic aspects of travel, and I was curious to see the boundary that had once been a simple internal division within the Soviet Union but had now become the fault line between the European Union and Russia: the unofficial border between East and West.

Mari's father came in and settled himself down in a scruffy armchair perpendicular to where I was sitting on my own. Strong words—I knew not their meaning—had been exchanged between him and the partygoers as they were leaving, and he looked at me and shrugged in the international language of male solidarity. I nodded back in an apologetic manner. We were about to bond.

And then it started. Question after question, fired at me in unintelligible Estonian. I tried in vain to explain that I couldn't understand—that we could not comprehend each other without speaking the same language—but it was to no avail. He would fix me with those piercing blue eyes, make some demand of me, and then throw his hands up in the air in exasperation when I failed to answer. It went on, the minutes dragging out into hours as he became increasingly agitated. And there was no escape, because only then did it occur to me that I had no idea where I'd be sleeping. In all the excitement of trampolines and horses I'd not even thought to ask which room I would be staying in that night.

He shuffled off to the kitchen, returning a short while later with a bottle of some suspect red-coloured spirit and a couple of shot glasses that he placed carefully on a small table in front of us. He poured two generous measures and motioned to me that I should drink. I gingerly picked up the glass and sniffed it. It smelled like a combination of paint stripper and methylated spirits, and as far as I could tell it probably was.

He took the glass and downed it in one gulp before reaching for the bottle for a refill. I had a sip: it was vile, like the worst kind of firewater you could imagine. Only one thing for it; make a small prayer, take a breath and swallow. I hoped to God I wouldn't be offered any more.

So it went on: Mari's father filling his glass to the brim and ingesting it in one fell swoop, me protesting that I wanted no more. And still came the questions and the exasperation and the accompanying sense of impending unease.

After what felt like an eternity he rose unsteadily to his feet and beckoned for me to follow. We stepped outside into the cool Estonian air; a few clouds streaked across the night sky, but between them I could see a field of stars that bathed the ground below in an ethereal glow. A distinctive smell of pine wafted over from the nearby forest, but what could have been magical under any other circumstances was completely lost on me now.

I followed the staggering figure to a dingy garage, where he hoisted up the door and turned on a light, the sort with a dangling string that you always see in the movies. It was filled with car parts, DIY tools and other assorted detritus—all the sorts of things you'd expect to find in an Estonian garage, I suppose.

On the wall was a large wooden rack with an assortment of tools—hammers, chisels and the like. The man reached behind the rack and grasped around in the darkness before emitting a satisfied sigh. He withdrew his hand slowly and purposefully. In his hand was a gun.

He looked at the rifle lovingly for a few moments before indicating that I should take it. It was heavy, really heavy; I put the sights to my eye and scanned the distant trees in a long slow arc, trying to imagine an unknown enemy hiding out there in the darkness. But I decided not to squeeze the trigger because I really didn't want to know if it was loaded.

I handed the gun back, nodding to show my appreciation at his generosity. He smiled with satisfaction and quietly stashed it back behind the tool rack, safe from the prying eyes of others.

Back in the living room, I was hoping that the experience with the gun in the garage, as unsettling as it was, might prove to be a turning point, a moment where Britain and Estonia had joined together in a display of international brotherhood. But it was not to be; out came the bottle once more, and once again came the interrogation.

All this time I hadn't heard anything from Mari's future sister-in-law since the partygoers had originally left; she had gone to bed with her daughter, and I'd been seriously considering waking them so that I could at least have someone there who might be able to calm the father a bit.

Suddenly he rose to his feet and stormed off into the kitchen, shouting at the top of his voice. Now I was scared, for it suddenly dawned on me that I was in a house somewhere in the middle of nowhere with an extremely drunk and volatile man who couldn't speak English and who kept a weapon hidden in his garage.

The mother of Mari's niece suddenly appeared. "Please," she said urgently. "Please. Protect my child. There is danger. I will get help." And then she left.

I decided there was only one thing to do. I texted Mari to ask for help and then went into the kitchen, where her father was pacing up and down and muttering to himself. "I, er, I go pee," I said, motioning with my zipper to get the point across. I glanced across to the room where the little girl was sleeping; fortunately the door was firmly closed.

The toilet was outside, so I hurried over to it and checked my phone. No reply. I scrolled to Mari's number and dialled. Please, please, pick up, please.

"Hello?" said a voice at the other end. "Mari!" I blurted out. "You have to come back, quickly. Your dad is going crazy over here; I don't know why, but I think he's drunk."

By the time Mari and her mother returned, I was still hiding outside, watching her father throwing crockery around the house. "I'm so sorry," said Mari as her parents argued in hurried Estonian. "He has this bad problem with alcohol. It's always been like this."

It was with some irony, then, that I found myself staying that night at the very friend's house whose party I had been denied entry to just a few hours before. The merrymaking was still in progress when I arrived in the early hours of the morning, a group of individuals of all ages sitting around a table packed high with nibbles.

The bed was one of the most comfortable I'd ever slept in.

In the morning I sat chatting to some of the people who'd been attending the birthday festivities. They were warm and lovely, some of the older ones apologising for their lack of English. I begged them not to worry, and apologised myself for my inability to speak Estonian. "It's okay," beamed one, "some people have been here sixty years and still can't speak Estonian!"

Outside, where an elderly dog lay on his back and demanded that I rub his tummy, I chatted with Mari. She was upset, and her tales of a childhood spent with an alcoholic parent were tinged with sadness. "It was one reason why I left," she said. "I honestly didn't think there was any alcohol in the house; I'm so sorry." I could bring myself to feel no anger at all.

Later that day Mari's brother drove us to the town of Rakvere, from where I'd be able to make my way to the Russian border. On the way we came across a car driving aimlessly backwards and forwards at the side of the road, wheels skidding at each touch of the brakes—Mari's father. With a deep sigh Mari got out of the car. "I have to drive him home," she said, and gave me a hug. I couldn't wait to see her again.

The sky had turned a dreary grey by the time the bus pulled into Narva. My couchsurfing host could no longer be considered as such; I had paid the price for my unreliability and he had gone away for the weekend. Instead I wandered around for a little bit, looking for a place to stay. On the way from the bus station I walked past what I took to be the crossing to Russia—men in uniform were certainly there, as well as barriers and stop signs, but I saw none of the menacing watchtowers or trigger-happy border guards that I'd so vividly imagined. I have to admit I felt a little disappointed.

At first glance, however, Narva appeared much as I'd expected it: uninspiring and a little depressing, the dismal weather adding to a somewhat sombre atmosphere. I was also surprised to see a distinct lack of the Cyrillic alphabet in the public realm; shop fronts, road names, signage and the like were largely in Estonian, despite this being very much a minority language in the town. Indeed, as if to make the point the few snatches of conversation I heard as I walked past some of the locals were exclusively of the Slavic persuasion.

I turned a corner and beheld the King Hotel, a respectable-looking faux-Bavarian edifice with a restaurant attached. I didn't want to search anymore so I decided there and then that it would have to do for the night. A bell rang as I pushed open the door and the young man at reception smiled warmly. "Zdrastvuytye," he said; "hello" in Russian.

My room was small and a little pokey, but it was acceptable. It had cost a princely sum but I consoled myself with the fact that this was the first time I'd shelled out for accommodation on the trip so far.

Now there are certain moments when all travellers start feeling jaded or fed up, or simply lose enthusiasm for the whole sorry thing. Sometimes the malaise can happen after weeks or months or even just a few days, and a whole host of things can cause it: perhaps the routine diet or tiredness, or a homesickness that has you wishing for the warm familiarity of your own bed. Whatever causes it, the main symptom is always the same: an increasing indifference to your surroundings and a diminishing return on the experience. To put it another way, travel can stop being fun. I'm not saying I was anywhere near that stage yet, but the previous night's antics in the Estonian countryside had left me feeling completely drained. I just couldn't build up any enthusiasm at the prospect of traipsing around town, so instead I decided to have a nap and worry about sightseeing later.

Such was my state a few hours later as I sat hunched over a piping-hot fruit tea in the hotel's restaurant, the lacklustre internet not making it as far as my room. In a couple of days I planned to be in Riga, the capital of neighbouring Latvia, and I weighed the options of staying in Narva for another night or pressing on elsewhere. I also took the opportunity to send off a few couchsurfing requests and to catch up on the news from home before turning in for the evening.

In the morning I felt refreshed and alive, the previous day's cobwebs having been thoroughly swept away by a great night's sleep. It was early morning and, after filling up on the King's idiosyncratic take on a continental breakfast, I set off to explore Narva with a spring in my step.

First stop was the town hall, in Raekoja plats—the one remaining baroque building in the centre of town, albeit heavily restored after its wartime destruction. The square itself was hardly worthy of the name: it resembled little more than a building site surrounded by Soviet-era Khrushcheby, the town hall itself a forlorn building that seemed all but abandoned. I took a couple of photos but it was more out of a sense of duty than for any aesthetic pleasure.

Khrushcheby are everywhere in the former Soviet Union. Built in large numbers from the premiership of Nikita Khrushchev onwards, these concrete blocks were initially intended to be a temporary solution to urban overcrowding but today hundreds of thousands of people still live in these buildings in Russia and farther afield. Most of them are no higher than five storeys, for the simple reason that Soviet health and safety laws required the installation of expensive lifts for buildings any taller. Halting construction five floors up often saved a substantial amount of cash.

This uniform blandness was famously satirised in a Soviet screwball comedy film from 1975 called *The Irony of Fate*. It tells the story of Zhenya Lukashin, a young Muscovite who gets hideously drunk with friends and instead of returning home to his fiancée for New Year's Eve is accidently put on a plane to Leningrad (present-day Saint Petersburg). After waking up in the city, and still thinking he is in the capital, he orders a taxi to take him to his home on 3rd Builders' Street—an address which also happens to exist in Leningrad. When he arrives the Khrushcheby looks exactly the same as Zhenya's block in Moscow, his key perfectly fits the lock of the apartment with the same number as his, and even the furniture is virtually identical. Zhenya is too drunk to notice and again falls asleep.

Later the real occupant of the flat, one Nadya Shevelyova, arrives to find a strange man in her bed. Cue a series of comic episodes as Zhenya attempts to leave the apartment but is forced to return repeatedly, Nadya's own fiancé arrives and assumes the worst, and unexpected guests turn up unannounced. Eventually Zhenya and Nadya are forced to spend New Year's Eve together, but their initial animosity soon dissolves and they begin to fall in love.

In the morning they realise they must part, and with a heavy heart Zhenya returns to Moscow. Once he has gone Nadya reconsiders everything that has happened and realises that she has let a chance at true happiness tragically slip away. She flies to Moscow, knowing that she'll find Zhenya easily since their addresses are both the same. It's a charming film with a subversive undercurrent, in the words of one critic an "explicit commentary…on the soulless uniformity of the Soviet urban landscape." It occupies a similar status in popular Russian consciousness as Frank Capra's *It's a Wonderful Life* does in the West and is broadcast across the former USSR every New Year's Day without fail.

I made my way towards the river, increasingly impressed with the way that the tedium of Narva's grey architecture and greyer skies were offset by a multitude of green lawns and leafy trees—a fact that had escaped me the day before and which was contributing to my growing warmth for the place. A short stroll from the town hall and this change of heart was cemented further with a fantastic vista as steep river banks swept down to the cold waters of Narva jõgi, the river that gives the town its name. And there, on the opposite bank, was Narva's Russian sister settlement of Ivangorod—my first-ever glimpse of the largest country on the planet.

A short distance over to the right was the "Friendship Bridge," an unremarkable structure except for the fact that it carries the main road from Tallinn to Saint Petersburg and is the only border crossing open to the public across the Narva River. A steady stream of pedestrian and vehicular traffic flowed across the bridge, and at the far end a large sign announced in big white letters that this was Russia—Россия—a fact that I found to be intensely exciting.

I also spied the twin fortresses that reinforce the notion that this river served as a border long before modern Estonia regained its independence. Founded by the Danes in the early thirteenth century and gifted to the Livonian Order a hundred years later, for centuries Narva marked the boundary between the Teutonic-ruled Baltic and subsequently Swedish Estonia in the west, and the nascent Russian state in the east. The building of Narva's castle on the western bank of the river was soon followed by the construction of the Tsarist Ivangorod fortress opposite, where they continue to glare at each other to this day.

And what a pair they were. On the right was the Estonian Hermann Castle, a squat edifice with a medieval-style tower looming high above the river; opposite was the hulking mass of Ivangorod, a lower but much larger fortress with a Russian flag atop one of its towers fluttering in the breeze. From here its walls looked utterly impregnable: a fitting metaphor, perhaps, for this vast and mysterious country.

Curiously, for a while both strongholds were actually in Estonia; during the interwar period the east bank of the Narva was also controlled by the Tallinn authorities, as defined in the terms of the Treaty of Tartu. In January of 1945, however, some territory of what was by now the Estonian Soviet Socialist Republic was ceded to Russia: a decision that, since these were internal Soviet boundary changes, had little real impact on day-to-day life. Come independence however and these shifting lines have become the new international border between the two countries, leaving part of former Estonia once again under Russian rule.

This isn't the only geographical curiosity in the area. Another anomaly lies farther south, on the other side of Lake Peipus. Here a small wedge of Russian land extends across a road connecting the two Estonian villages of Lutepää and Sesniki—the so-called Saatse Boot, named as such because of its boot-shaped appearance. It really is an oddity; travel between the two settlements means passing through a mile of Russian territory, and while no permits are required to drive its length it is completely forbidden to stop. Pedestrians are also prohibited, and any breach of these rules can be punished with temporary detention and a fine: Russian patrols have been known to hide along its length, eager to catch those who would breach these regulations. The area has even seen something of a miniature tourist boom in recent years as intrepid travellers come to visit one of the few places in Russia that can be entered without a visa.

According to legend the Boot owes its existence to a farm which for administrative purposes was included within the nearby Russian village of Gorodishche despite its proximity to its closer Estonian cousins. Once the Soviet Union fell, the new boundary blindly followed the somewhat arbitrary (but until that point relatively harmless) administrative line, ignoring the road that is now a part of the new Russia but that is connected to no other road within it. The government has thus far unsuccessfully attempted to trade ownership of the road for small patches of land elsewhere in south-eastern Estonia, but for now the Boot remains as enigmatic and curious as it was when it first came into existence.

It's not the only time when the question of where the border should actually be has reared its head. Few in modern Estonia have pressed for wholesale changes to the current boundary but some would still push for the restoration of Estonian sovereignty over the 2,000km2-odd territory that was annexed by Russia during the closing stages of the Second World War. Russia, on the other hand, completely rejects any such overtures and refuses to consider the Treaty of Tartu as having any contemporary legal status. Presumably, if the Estonian irredentists had their way, Ivangorod would once again become Jaanilinn, as it was known in the interwar period.

To make matters even more confusing, back in 1993 Narva and the surrounding district held a referendum on autonomy, potentially paving the way for unification with Russia. The narrow "yes" victory so alarmed the nascent Estonian authorities that they quickly acted to overrule the result, despite its backing by a certain former KGB lieutenant colonel by the name of Vladimir Putin. The campaign eventually petered out, but resentment at the Estonian government continues to fester in a town that prides itself in its Victory Day celebrations, a fact that hasn't gone unnoticed by Tallinn. Narva is now on the front line of an information war; growing paranoia at the creeping influence of Moscow's Russian-language media over the people of Narva has caused the national government to launch its own Russian television station to—in its own words—"bolster Estonia's psychological defences" against the creation of another frozen conflict.

The problem of shifting borders isn't unique to Estonia. During the chaos of war Latvia also lost a small amount of territory in the north-east of the country, whilst the boundaries of Lithuania were altered extensively in 1940 with the long-desired gain of Vilnius—a bittersweet compensation for Soviet occupation. The city, annexed by Poland two decades earlier, had been claimed by Lithuania since independence—indeed, its de *facto* capital Kaunas was officially designated as only fulfilling this role on a temporary basis until Vilnius's return to the fold. It was not a complete victory, however; some parts of the city's hinterland were transferred both to the Belarusian SSR (now the independent nation of Belarus) and to Nazi Germany, the latter subsequently gifted back to Poland at war's end as *that* country's borders were themselves shifted westwards.

In a similar vein, nearby Finland ceded huge amounts of land to the Soviet Union when both sides agreed to halt hostilities in 1944. A large swathe in the south-east of the country—including its second-largest city, Viipuri (modern-day Vyborg), and the strategically important Karelian Isthmus—was lost, as well as more remote Salla and Petsamo in the far north. The "Karelian Question," whilst not a dominant feature of contemporary Finnish politics, has never-the-less become something of a rally-ing cry for those who are eager to see the restoration of Finnish sovereignty over its historic lands.

Yet the main problem that nationalists in Finland and the Baltics face is that these lost lands have been extensive-ly Russified in the intervening years, their original popu-lations largely evacuated or expelled, to be replaced with resettled migrants from Russia in the Soviet authorities' deliberate (and ultimately successful) attempt to supplant the previous culture with their own. Narva's overwhelm-ing Russian majority is a direct result of this policy.

When you look at how much the map of Europe has changed over the last century it's perhaps not surprising that competing claims and contested space continue to this day all over the continent. Both world wars were particu-larly traumatic in this regard, with dismembered empires and fractured states contributing to an ever-growing list of nations. In place of the trio of Czechoslovakia, Yugoslavia and the USSR—all *bona fide* stamp-issuing countries in my childhood—some fifteen new European states have come into existence, with another in the guise of Kosovo yet to achieve full international recognition. And it may not yet be over; active separatist movements that are currently in full swing in the UK, Spain, France and elsewhere threaten to prolong a process of continuous fragmentation that may still not have reached its final conclusion.

I pushed these thoughts aside as I ambled to the castle, keen to take a closer peek at Narva's primary tourist draw. The sky was still dull, and as I came to the outside wall of the fortress and the heavy wooden door I saw a stone memorial, topped with a hammer and sickle encased in a red star. The dates on the column matched those of the Great Patriotic War.

More Soviet delights awaited in the courtyard. There, tucked around a corner of a building and largely out of sight was the first free-standing Baltic Lenin I'd clapped eyes on. He was striking a suitably dramatic pose, arm outstretched as if to proclaim the eternal glory of the Revolution. I noticed with a smile that his index finger was pointing in the direction of Russia.

The courtyard that Lenin now called home was deserted, but the castle looked even better in close up, its central tower flanked by sturdy stone fortifications—all that was missing were a few gallant knights on horseback, jousting for the attentions of a fair maiden. I was certain that given the devastation wrought on the town by the ebb and flow of marauding armies over the centuries some heavy restoration work must have gone on, but if so it had been done in a sympathetic and unobtrusive manner. I particularly liked the look of the wooden walkway at the very top, which promised great views over the surrounding landscape.

The castle plays host to the Narva Museum, and the two large bells outside the entrance hinted at the contents inside: lots of cannons, suits of armour and other assorted medieval bits and pieces, as well as a history of the town and its surroundings. Not all of the captions were in English but it wasn't always difficult to work out what the various items on display were, Narva's turbulent history and changes of ownership documented in a series of attractive miniature dioramas.

The real star of the show, however, was the castle itself; atmospheric narrow passageways opened into well-lit rooms and informative displays, with narrow staircases taking the visitor ever higher up the central tower. It struck me as a real jewel in an otherwise rather dishevelled crown, and I thought that it deserved to be busier.

The wooden walkway at the summit of the central tower did not disappoint; the views to the fortress on the opposite shore of the Narva River were stupendous, and in the distance Russia's unimaginable vastness stretched away into infinity. Ivangorod looked to be within a proverbial stone's throw, as if I could almost reach out and touch it. It felt strange being able to see into a country that was so close and yet so completely cut off. The resonance with the cultural division within Estonia was readily apparent.

It had occurred to me before I journeyed to the Baltics that the possibility of visiting Russia might arise given that I would be certain to travel to its border, but both the labyrinthine visa process and the risk of overstretching the project's brief had been enough to put me off. But as I scanned the horizon it seemed such a shame that I wouldn't be able to scurry across that bridge and explore my castle's twin across the river. It felt like an opportunity had been lost and it was strange that no one else had thought of the tourism potential in allowing the same sets of visitors to witness two monumental buildings that share an intimate and intertwined story. Seeing just one somehow didn't feel like the complete picture.

As it turns out, people have indeed made efforts in recent years to develop a joint tourist initiative; several projects such as the snappily titled "Development of the Unique Narva-Ivangorod Trans-Border Fortresses Ensemble as a Single Cultural and Tourist Object" have looked at developing a coordinated tourist infrastructure on both sides of the border. Yet the most obvious hindrance to the free movement of tourists is the border—and the visa restrictions that come with it.

I left Hermann Castle happy and saddened at the same time. I had a little time to kill before I had to return to the hotel to pick up my gear so I took in a few more sights, including the "Swedish Lion"—a replica of a 1930s monument commemorating Swedish monarch Charles XII's victory over the forces of the Tsar in 1701. I wondered what the local population thought of this interwar-era tribute to Russian military defeat.

As I made my way back to my hotel I considered my options for the rest of the day. The night before I had found another couchsurfing host in nearby Jõhvi, but in the morning I'd received a text cancelling my stay, and another night at the King would have eaten up most of that week's budget. One pleading message to Margit later and I had a bed for the night waiting for me in Tartu.

It transpired that this actually suited my plans rather well. My first stint in Estonia was shortly coming to an end; it was early May, and I wanted to be in Riga to coincide with Victory Day. Heading back to Tallinn and then striking south would have taken me along two sides of a rather large triangle, whereas a direct bus from Tartu would take me to Riga in half the time.

But there was no rush. By midday I was fully packed and waiting again at Narva's *bussijaam*, eager to see more of Estonia's Russian east. A glance at the map revealed two possibilities: a trip downriver to Narva-Jõesuu, where the great and good of Saint Petersburg society once congregated each year for concerts and fresh sea air, or to Sillamäe, a seaside settlement which promised to be a model of Stalinist architecture. Sillamäe just edged it, and half an hour later I was deposited by the side of the road, blinking in the glorious sunshine. The unexpected warmth was in complete contrast to the gloom that had permeated Narva just a short distance away.

The place's initial impressions continued to be favourable: standard grey-brick apartment blocks marched off into the distance and after only a short distance I came across a Soviet monument to what I assumed were Red Army pilots. I noted the fresh flowers lying at its base.

But the real treat was to be found farther down the main thoroughfare. Here was something that I'd not come across before in Estonia—elegant neoclassical Stalinist architecture, adorned with a hybrid mixture of Greco-Roman-Egyptian-style decoration with the occasional hammer-and-sickle or star motif thrown in for good measure. The main square, a beautifully landscaped park next to the temple-like Palace of Culture (which was sadly shut) had at its centre a statue of a muscular and bare-chested man holding what looked like the components of an atom whirling above his head.

A short distance away a once-elegant staircase, in need of a serious lick of paint, led me down a lovely tree-lined avenue flanked with more yellow-and-white buildings that gave the whole area a wonderful consistency of design. They all merited close inspection, the various symbols adorning their facades championing solid socialist values like industry and agriculture.

The reason that Sillamäe is a showpiece model town, rather than just another drab Soviet settlement, is because this was once a premier centre of uranium production that fed the USSR's nuclear-energy programme. Almost all of the inhabitants were at one time employed in the mine, which was closed down by the newly independent Estonian government in 1991.

Behind the well-proportioned structures lies a darker secret, however, and one that is costing both the local authorities and the European Union a great deal of money. Sillamäe's industrial legacy is a toxic mixture of radioactive waste that has slowly seeped into both sea and soil. This poisonous gift is visible from the stony beach just a short distance from the leafy boulevards, where large chimneys continue to dominate the horizon to the west of town. Needless to say, I didn't fancy a dip.

Margit seemed happy to see me, and truth be told I was happy to see her too. By the time I'd arrived back in Tartu and done a bit of shopping it was early evening, so we simply sat and talked over hot drinks in the comfort of her flat. "It's funny," she said, "I've never been to Narva. Or to Saaremaa, or Pärnu. I've travelled a lot in the world but there's still so much of Estonia I haven't seen yet."

My bus to Riga the next day was not until the afternoon, so I spent the morning having a final wander around Tartu's pleasant streets. Near the university I came across a statue to Jan Tõnisson, a prominent politician of the interwar period who had been at various times both prime minister and head of state during Estonia's first bout of independence. Famed for his almost forty-year rivalry with fellow politician Konstantin Päts, Tõnisson became leader of the democratic opposition during Päts's increasingly authoritarian rule in the mid-1930s. Tõnisson's reputation as a patriotic martyr was further cemented when he was arrested and subsequently "disappeared" shortly after the Soviet annexation, the authorities thinking little of his political opposition to the new regime. To this day no one knows exactly when, where or how he was killed.

Päts's legacy, on the other hand, is much more controversial, not least for his antidemocratic tendencies and (as some would see it) capitulation to the USSR during the crisis of 1939–40. More sympathetic commentators argue that Päts had little choice in giving in to Moscow's demands, his hand forced by his country's perilous position between the great powers of Germany and Russia.

Päts ended his days in a string of Russian psychiatric hospitals after the war, his detention purportedly justified on the grounds of his "persistent claiming of being the President of Estonia." As part of his rehabilitation during the nationalist revival in the dwindling days of the USSR his remains were brought back to Tallinn and reburied in Metsakalmistu Cemetery, and a previously confiscated statue was re-erected in his birthplace.

Among Päts's more curious ideas was for Estonian union with Finland, and although this dream never came to fruition his devotion to the notion of a "Greater Finland" continued throughout his various administrations. This is due in part to the strong cultural links between the two countries, and because their respective languages are part of the unusual Finno-Ugric language group which counts such exotics as Hungarian and Sami amongst its number. Most Europeans—including those in Latvia and Lithuania—speak Indo-European languages, and often find the multiple vowels that so characterise Estonian and Finnish fiendishly difficult to master.

This cultural affinity was perhaps best exemplified in the *Heimosodat*, or "Kinship Wars," that were fought as part of the Finno-Baltic theatre of the Russian Civil War. Between 1918 and 1922 some nine thousand Finnish volunteers, many of whom had fought against the Bolshevik army in order to secure Finland's independence, took part in various Finnic freedom movements inside Russian territory including Estonia and parts of nearby Karelia.

As I sped away to a new land and a new language I thought about the fortnight I'd spent in Estonia and of the people I'd met along the way. I'd seen just a small portion of the country but already I understood that this beautiful and beguiling place was full of contradictions, that the accepted image of this most progressive and advanced of the former Soviet states was tempered by its uneasy and sometimes controversial relationship with its Russian-speaking minority. And this time I didn't need Mari to tell me that I would be back; I already knew I would be.

CHAPTER 5

To Victory

* * *

NEAR THE CENTRE OF RIGA stands a large red granite statue of three men all dressed in military-style greatcoats,
inscribed *Latviešu Strēlnieki 1915–1920* at its base. The
monumental style is typical of the Soviet period, but what
makes this statue particularly interesting is the group it is
dedicated to: the "Latvian Riflemen."

Somewhat paradoxically the Riflemen were and continue to be worshipped as heroes by both Latvian nationalists
and Soviet loyalists alike. Created by the Russian authorities in 1915 to defend the empire against the encroaching
Germans, the regiment suffered huge losses on the front
and quickly became a byword for Latvian military prowess
and sacrifice. Subsequently angered at the inept military
leadership displayed by the Tsar, they proved to be ripe for
Bolshevik radicalisation and went on to play an instrumen-
tal role in the Russian Revolution. Lenin considered those
Riflemen who remained loyal to the (communist) Reds
at war's end the only revolutionary forces he could truly

trust, and they repaid that respect by successfully defending the Kremlin during an attempted coup against the new regime in 1918. Others fought to establish the short-lived Latvian Socialist Soviet Republic against former comrades who had sided with the (anti-communist) Whites and the wider independence movement.

In many ways the Riflemen perfectly encapsulate the contradiction at the heart of the Latvian nation: that with a Russian-speaking population approaching parity with Latvians in the capital and almost 30 per cent nationwide, Latvia has one of the most contested ethnic and cultural legacies in the Baltics.

I was staying at a hostel barely a minute's walk from the statue, a gaudy establishment by the name of Friendly Fun Franks and whose main entrance was tucked away on a small side street. It was deceptively big, its numerous rooms spread over a couple of floors and all painted in the same overly bright and slightly nauseating shade of orange.

The fact that I was lodging at Franks was no mere accident. Several years previously I had met a young Latvian by the name of Zane in a Leeds nightclub I was working in, and in the ensuing few months I got to know her and her circle of friends rather well. Zane, like so many of her contemporaries from Eastern Europe, had moved to the UK for work and excitement and seemed to have found both in Yorkshire's largest city.

Zane and her associates, it also transpired, all hailed from or near Riga and had largely met through the same employer—Friendly Fun Franks. And whilst Zane had decided that her future lay in Britain some of her former colleagues eventually drifted back to Latvia and one of them—Liga, whom I had known as the quiet one—had gone back to work at Franks.

I found her at the main reception, her flowing hair as magnificent as I'd remembered. It was certainly nice to see a familiar face, and as I exchanged coins for keys we promised that at some point during my stay we'd make time for a proper catch-up.

It was early evening, and after I'd been shown to my room and downed a complementary bottle of sweet beer in the hostel's bar—which appeared to be playing the same ice hockey game on a loop—I got to chatting with a group of young English lads who all worked for the same firm back home and who were enjoying their first trip to Latvia. They were a nice bunch, fun but not too rowdy, and it was interesting for me to listen to this new breed of tourist seeking out the lesser-known corners of Europe. "We're off shooting AK-47s tomorrow if you want to join us," offered one of them. I said I would think about it.

Instead I went for a short wander around town. My first impressions were favourable; I found a pleasing ensemble of medieval and baroque that together lent the place an air of wonderful consistency. It was a pleasant surprise, for Riga is by far the largest city in the Baltic states and the only one that might be considered approaching anything like a metropolis. Soviet grime was—at least in the centre of town—refreshingly absent, and in the warm summer air the narrow streets and bustling bars and restaurants were thronged with tourists and locals alike.

Yet in spite of this apparent renaissance Riga's population has steadily declined since Latvia's independence, from just under a million inhabitants a couple of decades ago to around seven hundred thousand today, primarily as a result of low birth rates and emigration to Western Europe. This wasn't yet a crash of crisis proportions, but Latvia's incorporation into the European Union appeared to have inadvertently hit the country hard demographically. Indeed, this was an issue right across the Baltics; in neighbouring Estonia, for example, the number of inhabitants peaked at 1.57 million in the (pre-independence) 1989 census. Fast-forward twenty years and the population had fallen to 1.29 million. And in Lithuania it's estimated that one in five people has been lost since the fall of Communism, and of those a disproportionate number are younger people who are seeking new opportunities elsewhere. While some of this drop in numbers is attributable to fewer births many think that immigration abroad has had the biggest impact, leading to fears in some quarters that a modern-day brain drain of increasingly epic proportions is taking place.

I vividly remember the scare stories in the media when the European Union expanded eastwards. Much was made of the then British government's woeful underestimation of the numbers of people who were migrating to the UK looking for work and a better standard of living. The over-whelmingly right-wing press had a field day, with tales of migrants taking all our jobs *and* sponging off benefits—although how they were managing to do both. And the usual suspects—the Tories, the Daily Mail and so on—were able to play to people's base fears without undertaking what I felt to be a real analysis of the situation, which I always suspected was at least partly intentional.

You see, this was a new type of migration for a new century. Many of the people who came did so on a purely temporary basis, earning money and sending it to their families before rejoining them back home some time later. And those who stayed tended to assimilate relatively quickly. Zane, fluent in English and forming lasting relationships with the indigenous population, was a case in point.

These thoughts aside, I also found the Riflemen standing incongruously in what was now essentially a car park, but back in the early 1990s this place had been the focal point of pro-communist demonstrations; the flowers at its base told of its continuing significance to at least some of the city's populace. It would seem that independence wasn't, and continues not to be, welcomed by all sections of society. I was tired however and I'd had enough for the night, but already I couldn't wait to see more of Riga over the next few days.

The journey from Tartu had been a smooth one, on a modern and comfortable coach that had originated in

Saint Petersburg and was therefore carrying a largely Russian contingent. It was fairly quiet and I had a double seat to myself—always a luxury in bus travel—and I amused myself by watching the incredibly dull news programme playing on a television screen above the driver. One of the more animated highlights was "Estonian trade minister says Estonian-Russian export figures may be inflated." You get the gist.

At the border we stopped briefly in Valga. Valga is unusual, because the border between Estonia and Latvia runs straight through the middle of town and going from one side to the other once entailed a lengthy trip through passport control. Now both countries are part of the Schengen free movement zone and today there is unimpeded travel between the two, a situation no doubt appreciated by the local populace. I wasn't even sure of the exact moment when we crossed the line.

Being a fan of geographical oddities it was rather exciting to be here. Valga—or Valka, as it's known on the smaller Latvian side of town—was a prime example of the new and sometimes unexpected divisions that were created at the time of the Soviet Union's demise. What was once a mere internal boundary within the same country had suddenly metamorphosed into an international border, replete with all the guards and fences and bureaucracy that that immediately entails. In the chaos of independence families were torn apart and people were barred from seeing their loved ones. Membership of the European Union has largely solved this problem in the Baltics—aliens, of course, notwithstanding—but elsewhere in the former USSR people often experience considerable difficulty in crossing from one jurisdiction to another when, prior to independence, such a crossing would have been as simple as crossing a street.

The current Belarus-Lithuania border is but one example. What was once just a dashed line on a map is now a physical barrier dividing the two states, and villagers in neighbouring settlements like Norviliškės (Lithuania) and Piackuny (Belarus) can only communicate with one another over a fence. Actually gaining permission to cross to the other side entails a fifty-mile round-trip to the nearest visa-issuing office. It's almost as if the barriers that came down with the end of the Cold War never actually disappeared at all—they merely shifted slightly eastwards.

Later that night I found that I was sharing my room with an Australian. We chatted about his travels around Europe but I found the conversation stilted and a little forced, so after a while I let him be. I was just glad that I had thought to bring ear plugs, for the unwritten rule that hostels will always allocate at least one extravagantly loud snorer to every room had once again proved entirely accurate.

The sun was blazing in a glorious blue sky as I made my across Akmens Tilts—literally "Stone Bridge"—and over to the opposite bank of the Daugava River that splits Riga clean in two. It's a big, broad sluggish river, and in the distance I could make out one of the many cruise ships that stop in the Latvian capital during their regular circuits around the Baltic.

It was still fairly early, but I was no mere solitary figure; a veritable exodus was moving in the direction of a thin sliver of a monolith that lay enticingly on the horizon. Traffic heaved and pulsated on the wide boulevard and trams rumbled down the middle, with pedestrians spilling from the pavements taking care to avoid the wheels of both.

Soon a large green expanse opened up, a lovely park sprinkled with trees. Under the shade of a few of them archetypal *babushkas* were selling bright flowers from rough homemade stalls, their trade brisk as families, couples, young and old, all stopped to pick out the most colourful bunch.

By the time I reached the Soviet Victory Memorial— or the "Monument to the Liberators of Soviet Latvia and Riga from the German Fascist Invaders," to give it its official title—I was virtually pushing my way through the crowds. The monument itself was suitably grand, with large gold star-topped pillars of concrete flanked on either side by a group of soldiers and an allegory of Mother Russia, but instead my eye was drawn to the displays that lined its approaches. Here officers dressed in period Soviet uniforms were reclining against small tanks and armoured cars or sat drinking tea out of samovars, just as their forebears might have done at the front. Others demonstrated how to use some of the decommissioned weapons on display or took part in animated discussions with visitors in front of the many photographs and documents that were on show.

Loud music was pumping from a stage near the memorial's edge, and as I got closer I could see that the crowd was carefully piling a vast ocean of flowers in front of it. Carpets of reds and yellows covered the ground and all around, every single bulb placed purposefully in a ceremony of utmost respect. Others chose to give their flowers to some of the elderly veterans who were mingling with the crowds, their pristine uniforms invariably weighed down with medals clinking gently in the breeze.

Traditional music and dancing of a folksy sort was taking place on the stage, conjuring up idyllic images of a rural Russia peopled by peasants living simple and pure lives. As I wandered through the crowds taking pictures the entertainment gave way to speeches, the content of which I could only guess at but which were universally greeted with claps and cheers.

Behind the monument was a small lake; together they formed a large hexagon. A path took me around the edge, along numerous food stalls from which hunger-inducing smells wafted over everybody. In the lake itself two policemen splashed around in a little rowing boat in a somewhat comical and—it has to be said, given the lack of discernible water-borne security concerns—rather pointless fashion.

But what really struck me was that everything about the event was overtly Soviet, from the red flags and banners to the overwhelming absence of any Latvian symbols, heritage or language. The only indication that this was taking place in what was now another country was a discreet line of small Latvian flags fluttering at the monument's edge. Indeed, for some this acknowledgement is not enough: two members of an ultranationalist Latvian group were killed in an unsuccessful bomb attack on the monument in 1997.

When you look at the origins of Victory Day this is perhaps not surprising. All across the former USSR the defeat of the Nazi menace is celebrated annually on 9 May, the day after its counterpart is marked in Western Europe (by the time the "German Instrument of Surrender" had been signed it had already past midnight in Moscow). Since then, and depending on whom you ask, the commemoration of the Great Patriotic War has been a celebration of either the Red Army's heroic blood sacrifice or the beginning of Soviet occupation.

This fact has frequently hampered relations between the new Russia and the Baltics ever since the disintegration of the Soviet state. The presidents of Lithuania and Estonia flatly refused to attend the sixtieth anniversary ceremonies in Moscow, declaring them incompatible with their respective nations' experiences under Soviet rule, and it's unlikely that the presence of divisive domestic festivities will change that policy any time soon. What is certainly clear is that Victory Day—at least in the Baltics—has mutated from a commemoration of war's end and the defeat of fascism into a defiant celebration of Russian identity.

As if to make that point a convoy of cars, many of them sporting Russian and Soviet flags, were making slow circuits around the park with horns blaring as they went. Each was daubed with Cyrillic slogans and hammer-and-sickle emblems, and even with my very limited grasp of the language I could make out phrases like "Thank you, veterans!" and "Hooray! Victory!"

There is, of course, a delicious irony in all this. The regime that ground down Germany on the Eastern Front and arguably contributed more to the war effort than any other country is of course no more, the twin dangers of economic and political stagnation doing the job that Hitler so notably failed to achieve.

As I journeyed back into town I noticed that many in the crowd wore ribbons of vertical black-and-orange stripes pinned to their clothing or in their hair, and although I didn't understand its meaning at the time it transpired that this is the Ribbon of Saint George, one of the most recognised and respected symbols of Russian military valour and a symbol that is closely associated with the Second World War. I was to see this symbol frequently on display throughout the "Russian" Baltic, its intention no doubt to signify a cultural affinity with both Russia and the Russian-speaking diaspora. That day it was easy to spot who was Russian and who was not in the Latvian capital.

CHAPTER 6

The Language
of Freedom

* * *

LATER THAT EVENING I CHATTED with the girl behind
the bar at Franks, a Latvian by the name of Viktorija who
seemed quite pleased to have a distraction on what was
otherwise a slow night.

"So you're sure you don't mind me taking up some of
your time?" I enquired, in the way of the man who doesn't
get the chance to chat up dusky beauties very often. "I
know you must have a lot of glasses to clean, or whatever it
is you have to do when it's so quiet in here." She laughed,
tossing her hair in an endearingly self-conscious fashion.
I'm sure getting hit on in such an obvious fashion was a
regular occurrence.

"No, it's fine. It's not exactly like I'm busy at the moment; actually it's nice to have someone to talk to. So
where are you from?"

I explained that I was born in London, had moved to
Norfolk when I was young, attended school in Lincolnshire,

spent summer holidays in North Wales, attended university in Leicester, made the move north to Leeds, crossed the Irish Sea to Belfast, spent a year on the continent in Brussels, and was now back in Belfast. I had to admit that I quite enjoyed reeling this list off, as if it made me somehow exotic.

"Wow, that's a lot, you really are a traveller!"

"Ha, yes, most of my friends would tell you that I get around a bit. But they mean the moving, of course."

I think the euphemistic joke was lost on her but she smiled anyway.

"So, did you enjoy Riga today?" she asked.

"Yes, very much, I can't believe how nice the weather has been. Actually, it's been really good ever since I started this trip; I've not seen any rain at all. People won't believe me when I say I've been to the Baltic countries after I come back with a suntan."

"Ah just wait, I'm sure we'll have some bad weather eventually. Often when it's sunny like this for a long time we get thunderstorms. But yes, this is really good weather at the moment. Such a shame I have to be stuck at work! So are you just travelling around Latvia, then? What are your plans?"

I explained the purpose of my trip and told her about my adventures in the Estonian countryside. At the end she frowned.

"It sounds interesting. What made you think of this topic? Did you know that the Soviets used alcohol as a weapon—to make Baltic people more pliable and easy to control? So I guess you must have gone to the celebrations today at the memorial?"

"I did, yes. I found it very interesting. I mean, it felt very Russian. It's the first time I've been to Victory Day, so I wasn't exactly sure what to expect. I've heard that it can be controversial here in Riga as well. But everyone there seemed to enjoy it: to be happy, I mean." I paused for a moment. "But I understand that not everyone in the city would feel comfortable there."

"You're right, not everyone would," Viktorija nodded. "I am mixed; I have Latvian and Ukrainian parents so I am not fully Latvian, and I speak Russian as well. But I do not agree with the way Victory Day is celebrated here. I mean, I have nothing against remembering the people who died in the war. But this day is more than that now; it's a celebration of the Soviet Union. And Soviet times were bad in Latvia."

As she spoke Liga had wandered in, sidling up next to Viktorija and nodding in agreement with what she was hearing. "I would never go to Victory Day," she said decisively at the end.

A short while later fireworks lit up the horizon on the opposite bank of the Daugava, coming from the direction of the Soviet Monument. "Russian fireworks," said Liga drily, her thinly veiled disgust dripping with disapproval. I said nothing in return.

I had interviews planned for the following day, but shortly after my arrival in Riga both my contacts asked to rearrange. In truth I didn't mind; the sun was still shining, and so I took the opportunity to get to know this intriguing place a little bit better.

The first stop was the Museum of the Occupation of Latvia, an ugly, squat rectangular hulk that once housed a museum dedicated to the Latvian Riflemen and that stands directly behind the eponymous monument. In an unabashed sign of the times, the building was converted shortly after independence in the early 1990s to document Latvia's treatment by the Soviet and Nazi regimes. Now a grey-green rust colour, it had apparently once been red to reflect the ideological sympathies of its subjects at the time.

Inside the tone was not dissimilar to that of its sister in Tallinn. Portraits of Hitler and Stalin hung ominously above the entrance, the leaders held directly responsible for the travails of the Latvian nation during the latter half of the twentieth century. Photographs, posters and other assorted objects told a depressingly familiar story of random arrests, mass deportations, executions and other dubious methods of state repression.

Perhaps most engaging was a mock-up of a Siberian gulag barrack block that was used to house prisoners whom the authorities considered to be in some way politically or culturally deviant, or who had simply been in the wrong place at the wrong time. It had cramped bunk beds that one could imagine would have been infested with lice and a "toilet" that was no more than a steel barrel in a corner.

Its foul stench would have been absolutely unimaginable. It was clear that these conditions would be entirely unsuitable for any semblance of dignified human habitation.

And yet these prisoners would somehow make do. Items dotted around the cabin included painstakingly handmade Christmas cards, chess sets made out of beautifully carved wood, and makeshift balaclavas recycled from old scraps of material in a futile effort to ward off the cold. The bleakness of their existence must have been close to unendurable.

The gulag was, of course, one of the Soviet Union's most infamous creations. A huge system of forced labour camps that housed prisoners from all walks of life, the Gulag entered the West's collective consciousness in Aleksandr Solzhenitsyn's celebrated work *The Gulag Archipelago*. In it the author likens the scattered camps to a chain of islands: a deliberate and systematic instrument of political repression that spanned the entire length of this gigantic, frozen land. He suggested that the Soviet government could not govern without the threat of imprisonment and that the economy itself depended on the productivity of the camps. Solzhenitsyn himself spent several years in various camps after criticising Stalin's war strategy in private correspondence to a friend; he based the work on his own experiences and those of others.

Archipelago was only one of several forays that Solzhenitsyn made into the world of the Gulag. His novel *One Day in the Life of Ivan Denisovich*, which describes a typical day in the life of an ordinary camp inmate, caused a sensation when it was published in 1962 in the Soviet literary magazine *Novy Mir* (*New World*). It was the first account of Stalinist repression to be openly distributed in the country and Solzhenitsyn would go on to win the 1970 Nobel Prize for Literature, be expelled from the USSR in 1974 (a year after the publication of *Archipelago*), and finally return to Russia some twenty years later. He died in 2008 at the age of eighty-nine, a legacy of opposition to the Soviet regime marred in his later years by accusations from some quarters of anti-Semitism chiefly as a result of his history of Jews in the Russian Empire titled *Two Hundred Years Together.*

Needless to say, conditions in the camps were profoundly harsh: flimsy clothing, overcrowding, poorly insulated housing, poor hygiene, and scant health-care provision were all a daily reality. Inmates often had to work in shocking conditions using entirely inadequate equipment. Perhaps most brutal was the "you-eat-as-you-work" system, where inmates' rations were dictated by their work output. Amazingly, it was a prisoner who had allegedly recommended this policy; so impressed were the authorities that he was soon promoted to camp commander.

Perhaps taking inspiration from the traditional Tsarist punishment of exile that preceded it, the numbers of people who passed through the Gulag system (or indeed how many perished) is unknown. Even the most conservative estimates range in the millions. Prisoners were not just those who had offended the Soviet state; dissidents would often find themselves mixed with common criminals, assorted deviants and—as in the case of the Baltics—ethnic minorities whom the authorities thought posed a risk to the state. The name "Gulag comes from the Russian acronym for *Glavnoye upravleniye lagerey i koloniy*, or "Main Camp Administration." Often the camps had no walls, because they didn't need to; they were so remote and so isolated that escape would have been impossible. To describe the conditions of inmates as slave labour would not be an exaggeration.

The museum's owners also were not subtle in expressing their views about the post-war arrivals from elsewhere in the USSR; my guidebook claimed that the "Soviets tried to rob Latvia of its ethnic identity" and this message was reinforced throughout. On industrialisation: "The necessary labour is brought from the Soviet Union in a deliberate attempt to reduce the Latvian proportion of the population." On culture: "Restrictions [were in place] on the use of the Latvian language and the promotion of Russian...there was Sovietisation of all sections of society." And Russian immigration into Latvia was declared to be "colonisation."

Such accusations, I was fast learning, were not uncommon in the contemporary Baltics; an official Estonian government website I had stumbled on shortly before my trip to the museum described the "outrageous migration policies essential to the Soviet Nationalisation programme aiming to Russify Estonia—forceful administrative and military immigration of non-Estonians from the USSR coupled with the mass deportations of Estonians to the USSR." While there might be an element of truth in some of these assertions it did make me wonder if a Russian speaker reading this might be justified in questioning his or her allegiance to the new countries that were created in the wake of the Soviet Union's collapse.

And, just as in Tallinn, there was very little mention of the men who had signed up to the Nazi cause. The only hint at local enthusiasm for their German liberators was a photograph of young Latvian women in national costume greeting swastika-bedecked soldiers with flowers and smiles, which in any case neatly sat with the museum's anti-Soviet theme. This was something of an omission, because the legacy of the Latvian Legion can still be felt today.

In Latvia, as was the case throughout the occupied territories in the east, the Nazis formed local regiments of Waffen-SS troops to supplement their own forces fighting the Russians on the Eastern Front. In the case of Latvia this was undertaken primarily by conscription, but the core of the Legion was made up of members of the notorious Arajs Kommando, a native Latvian police unit that became one of the most efficient and effective killing units during World War II.

The Kommando actively participated in a number of atrocities including the killing of Jews, Roma, communist partisans and civilians, primarily along Latvia's remote border with the Soviet Union but also at Liepāja on the coast and elsewhere. Perhaps most infamous was its involvement in the mass execution of Jews expelled from the Riga ghetto and of Jews deported from Germany in the Rumbula massacre near the Latvian capital. According to some estimates, in total the Kommando may have murdered around twenty-six thousand people of the Jewish faith.

And yet the question of whether the actions of the Legion constitute war crimes is still highly controversial. Some historians maintain that it was merely a front-line combat unit, rather than an Einsatzkommando-style death squad, and as organisations that were largely made up of conscripts the Allies viewed Baltic regiments far more favourably at the end of the war. To date no Latvian has ever been convicted of a war crime whilst serving as a member of the Legion, but the presence of Arajs Kommando and the indigenous fascist movement Pērkonkrusts amongst its members has done much to tarnish the Legion's reputation as mere victims of circumstance. This contemporary lack of recognition of local collaboration in Nazi atrocities was for me most pointedly summarised by a tiny and suspiciously half-hearted display in the Genocide Museum in Vilnius that blithely acknowledged that "the Nazis managed to involve some of the local residents in these crimes."

In the chaos of war, however, even national heroes do unspeakable things. Take the case of Herberts Cukurs:

born in Liepāja at the dawn of the twentieth century, Cukurs became a pioneering long-distance pilot during the golden age of aviation in the 1930s, forging routes to places as far afield as Gambia and Japan. In 1933 the dashing Cukurs claimed the prestigious Harmon Trophy for aviation.

But then the war came. In the summer of 1941, when the occupation of the Baltics by Nazi Germany was complete, Cukurs joined the Arajs Kommando and would go on to take a leading role in atrocities at Riga and Rumbula. By the time of the second Soviet invasion he had earned himself the unenviable epitaph the "Butcher of Riga," who was held personally responsible for the deaths of thousands of Latvia's Jews.

Cukurs was able to make his escape amid the chaos of the German retreat from the Baltics, fleeing to South America, where he set up an aviation business in São Paulo that by all accounts he operated with no attempt to hide his identity. In February 1965 he was lured to the Uruguayan capital of Montevideo on the pretence of a business proposal and was assassinated by Israeli Mossad agents. A note was sent to media outlets stating: "Taking into consideration the gravity of the charge levelled against the accused, namely that he personally supervised the killing of more than thirty thousand men, women and children…the accused Herberts Cukurs is hereby sentenced to death. Accused was executed by those who can never forget."

What is beyond dispute is that the Legion saw intense action during the Siege of Leningrad and the Eastern Front before splitting in two, with one division transferring to Prussia and the other remaining in what would become known as the Courland Pocket in western Latvia. There the latter, surrounded by Soviet forces, became one of the last Axis battalions to surrender, doing so on the ninth of May 1945: forever after known as Victory Day. Some of the soldiers would go on to become Forest Brothers.

The main reason this all remains relevant is that every year on 16 March Latvian ultranationalist groups hold commemorations to honour the Legion and its surviving veterans. In the capital this takes place at the Freedom Monument, a symbolic allegory of Latvian nationhood near the centre of the city that was constructed during the first era of independence. In recent years Latvian Legion Day has been particularly confrontational as demonstrations and counterdemonstrations supporting or protesting the event respectively take place amid a heavy security presence. The Latvian parliament—the *Saeima*—even made the day an official day of remembrance in the late 1990s, but soon bowed to international pressure to remove this formal recognition. The Council of Europe has even requested that "the Latvian authorities condemn all attempts to commemorate persons who fought in the Waffen SS and collaborated with the Nazis…[and] recommends that the authorities ban any gathering or march legitimising in any way Nazism." So far this condemnation has not been forthcoming.

Attempts have also been made to rehabilitate the likes of Cukurs. In 2005 an exhibition in Liepāja entitled "Herberts Cukurs: The Presumption of Innocence" sought to absolve him of any blame for the killings carried out by Arajs Kommando. And his execution without trial—unlike that most famous of anti-Nazi Mossad operations, the kidnapping and prosecution of Adolf Eichmann—has further entrenched his martyrdom in the eyes of the Latvian far right. When institutions like the Latvijas Okupācijas Muzejs skim or omit this history altogether, I can't help thinking that it's tantamount to collusion.

I did learn something new in the museum, however. Interestingly, and as is the case with Estonia, Latvia's initial incorporation into the USSR was only recognised by—somewhat ironically, given subsequent events—Nazi Germany and neutral Sweden. The latter, lying directly across the Baltic Sea, became the primary goal for thousands of refugees in the ensuing months and years. The United States, United Kingdom and several other nations regarded the annexation as illegal and, despite acknowledging de facto Soviet rule at the Yalta Conference of 1945, this tacit acknowledgement never translated into full legal recognition.

It's perhaps surprising then that to this day the Kremlin denies any suggestion that it acted without the full consent of the countries concerned. I say "surprising," because even during the lifetime of the USSR Soviet officials did acknowledge some of the wrongs that had been committed under Stalin's direction. The final collapse would, at least in theory, have allowed the new Russian authorities to distance themselves from what had been the legacy of a regime that no longer existed. But, as with Victory Day, Russia considers itself to be the direct inheritor of the Herculean Soviet war effort. With some justification one could argue—and nationalist historians almost always do—that to this day the contemporary condition of the Baltics was decided the moment Molotov and Ribbentrop signed their eponymous pact.

The museum itself is situated on the edge of the Rātslaukums, or Town Hall Square, dominated at one end by the Town Hall and at the other by the Gothic-style House of the Blackheads. The latter is quite an achievement, for despite its distinctively medieval look it's barely a decade old: while the original was partially destroyed by the invading Germans in 1941 the Soviets finished the job at the end of the war. Reconstructed just in time for Riga's 800th anniversary celebrations, it's a typical example of the rebuilding that has taken place in towns and cities once scarred by the twin terrors of war and bland socialist architecture. It reminded me a little of Warsaw, whose Old Town was faithfully reconstructed after being reduced to rubble.

I walked through central Riga's charming back alleys, which still retain much of their medieval charm thanks to a pleasingly jumbled array of buildings and an enviable lack of traffic. Tourists thronged the stalls and shops in the warm summer air; Riga was bustling, the excitement palpable. I had a list of various sites that I wanted to see and I took them all in—the cathedral, the Palace of Peter the Great, the Great and Small Guilds, the Three Brothers. Even the names were enough to conjure up images of tales of old: of knights of the Teutonic Order and the Hanseatic League that once dominated ancient Livonia.

In fact so enamoured was I with the Old Town—which, like the two other Baltic capitals is a UNESCO World Heritage site—that I almost forgot the purpose of my visit. So it was that I ducked into the Museum of the Barricades, a tiny establishment located past an anonymous door down a side street and up some roughly hewn steps. It was a treat. Inside a Soviet-era apartment had been fully restored—replete with dated wallpaper and furnishings to match—as well as a recreation of part of a barricade and memorials to those who had been killed.

The barricades were a seminal event in the push for Latvian independence. Having witnessed the brutal storming of the Vilnius Television Tower in neighbouring Lithuania in January 1991, where fourteen unarmed protesters were killed or mortally wounded by the Red Army, and fearful of a similar occurrence at home, nationalist protesters began to erect barriers to protect key targets mainly in Riga but also in other towns across the country. Anything that could be used to block the streets was utilised—vehicles, machinery, concrete, rubble, construction waste, logs, and wire. Over a period of about two weeks thousands worked in shifts to ensure that the barricades were permanently manned; six people were killed by pro-Soviet militia. Some 300 foreign journalists were also there to record the event, beaming images of popular resistance to a worldwide audience.

The problem partly stemmed from the fact that the Baltics had declared their independence unilaterally with no agreement from Moscow, which (not unreasonably, given the circumstances) the three states assumed would not be forthcoming. Lithuania was the first in the entire USSR, doing so on March 11 1990; Estonia and Latvia quickly followed, on 25 March and 4 May respectively. This meant that until official Soviet recognition came over a year later in September 1991 the countries were in a kind of constitutional limbo, with Moscow insisting that such declarations were illegal while the local authorities in Estonia, Latvia and Lithuania begging to differ. After the incidents in Riga and Vilnius the Communist Party gradually began to accept the inevitable, caught up as it was in dealing with an ever-increasing state of anarchy across the entire country. The August Coup of that year signalled the beginning of the end of the Soviet Union, and when the USSR State Council rubber-stamped Baltic independence one month later barely a whimper of protest could be heard.

All of this, of course, took place in the context of the turmoil that had engulfed the Soviet Union during the previous decade, which itself had its roots in the stagnation that had slowly developed years before. When Stalin finally died in 1953 the ensuing power struggle saw Nikita Khrushchev take power. Khrushchev famously denounced the excesses of his predecessor and led the country through a period known as "de-Stalinisation" that ushered in relatively liberal reforms including the dismantling of the Gulag system and the partial liberalisation of the arts in which (some) criticism of the regime was tolerated.

It was not to last. Communist Party colleagues, concerned at Khrushchev's policies and what they saw as his increasingly erratic behaviour, summoned him to a meeting in October 1964 and dismissed him. Khrushchev didn't put up a fight; in a phone call to a friend and colleague later that evening he opined: "Could anyone have dreamed of telling Stalin that he didn't suit us anymore and suggesting he retire? Not even a wet spot would have remained where we had been standing. Now everything is different. The fear is gone, and we can talk as equals. That's my contribution."

Khrushchev was replaced by Leonid Brezhnev, an instinctively conservative leader who revoked many of his predecessor's reforms during his eighteen-year rule, ushering in a period of economic, political and social inertia that developed into an ever-deepening malaise. It was at this time that writer Aleksandr Zinovyev popularised the term *Homo Sovieticus*—pliant, passive individuals who were indifferent both to the system that ruled over them and to the results of their labour, lacking in initiative and avoiding risk, and unable to think critically; all the result of the Soviet system.

Indeed, some would argue that the planned economy, with its lack of free-market forces and the profit motive, was deeply flawed and doomed to failure from the very beginning. Others cite the nation's high expenditure on defence—the USSR had the largest military of any country in the world at the time of its collapse—as a key cause of stagnation: no significant reforms were initiated during Brezhnev's tenure, and the few that were proposed were either extremely modest or were opposed by the majority of the Soviet leadership. Still others would suggest the repression of dissidents and the embrace of a gerontocracy as outward vestiges of a system that was slowly rotting from the inside; by the beginning of the 1980s the average age of a Politburo member was seventy years old.

Whatever the causes, by the time of Brezhnev's death in 1982 the Soviet Union he handed over to his successor was a country that was arguably far less dynamic than it was when he had assumed power. The continued prioritising of the military over consumer goods had created conditions in which the standard of living for ordinary citizens saw little real improvement, particularly when compared to the other great superpower of the time, the United States. Arts and literature became paralysed, to the point where artists who propagated Soviet values were favoured and those who did not—like Solzhenitsyn, or Andrei Sinyavsky and Yuli Daniel—were exiled or (in the case of Sinyavsky and Daniel) prosecuted via show trial solely for their literary output. Many found that the only way to publish their writings was either to have them smuggled abroad or clandestinely copied and distributed by hand using primitive tools and materials—the *samizdat* ("self-published"). The very fabric of society had become static.

Brezhnev's successor, former KGB head Yuri Andropov, attempted to arrest this stagnation by rooting out corruption; during his time in office he dismissed eighteen ministers and dozens of other senior party officials. The economic malaise was also acknowledged in public for the first time and he also made overtures towards reducing military spending by exploring options for a potential withdrawal from Afghanistan—a war frequently likened to the United States' involvement in Vietnam—although relations with the Reagan administration remained tense and arms-control talks ultimately collapsed.

Unfortunately Andropov was also a fully paid-up member of the gerontocracy who died at the age of sixty-nine after just fifteen months in post. The next general secretary, Konstantin Chernenko, lasted for an even shorter period of time, dying just over a year later at the age of seventy-three, chiefly as the result of a lifetime of heavy smoking. Towards the end he was confined to a hospital bed, barely able to speak; party officials applied a facsimile of his signature to all orders and correspondence. He was the third Soviet leader to die in fewer than three years.

Something needed to be done. A young, forward-thinking politician, at fifty-four Mikhail Gorbachev was the first leader of the Soviet Union to have been born after Lenin's October Revolution. Barely a year after he took power he launched the twin policies that would go on to define his premiership—*perestroika* ("restructuring") and *glasnost* ("openness").

Perestroika and glasnost were Gorbachev's attempt to overhaul and rejuvenate the Soviet political and economic systems. Modest reforms designed to transform the Soviet command economy into something more market-oriented were introduced in an attempt to better meet the needs of consumers; the emphasis on transparency aimed to tackle corruption and to permit a limited form of democracy in the guise of multicandidate elections for local Communist Party positions. Restrictions on the freedom of religion were eased and there was a thaw in the cultural arena; previously banned books such as George Orwell's *Nineteen Eighty-Four* and *Animal Farm* were made freely available for the first time. Gorbachev also carried out the biggest (albeit nonlethal) purge of the military since Stalin's day, replacing much of the old guard with officers promoted on merit. All of this was a huge departure from the Brezhnev era.

For conservatives such reforms were alarming in their scale and scope; for liberals, they weren't happening anywhere near fast enough. What is certain is that Gorbachev's transformations unintentionally became one of the primary catalysts for the dissolution of the Soviet Union. Glasnost permitted open criticism of the regime for the first time in two decades, while Perestroika proved to be a Pandora's box, exacerbating existing tensions and fanning the flames of nationalist discontent among the various republics. The Baltic states were at the forefront of that disquiet.

Not far from the Museum of the Barricades is the Freedom Monument, dedicated to the soldiers killed during the Latvian war of independence; as such, it's both the focal point of Latvian Legion Day and an embodiment of the national aspirations of the Latvian people. Its location in a pedestrianised plaza is enhanced by the way that it seems to suddenly open out as you emerge from the narrow streets of the Old Town. It really is a striking edifice, built in a handsome modernist style that is in complete contrast to the brutalist Soviet war memorial on the other side of the river.

I ambled around its red-and-white granite base, taking a few photos and admiring the reliefs of the Latvian cultural heroes that shone in the bright summer sun. On closer inspection I could see that its surface was heavily pockmarked, the victim of a combination of rain and air pollution, vibrations from the surrounding traffic and moss and lichens. Some shoddy restoration work over the years has done much to hinder rather than help efforts to save it, and locals have expressed considerable concern that much of the damage is irreversible. The monument has also been the recipient of unwelcome attention of another kind in recent years; in 2008 a drunken British tourist was jailed for five days for urinating at its base, sparking off a minor diplomatic incident.

At the front of the monument were the words *Tēvzemei un brīvībai* ("For Fatherland and Freedom"), which in turn drew my eye up along the long slender column that soared some fifty feet into the air. At its top a green-copper statue of Liberty stood proud, her arms stretched high above her head. In her hands were three gold stars, each symbolising one of Latvia's three historic regions—Kurzeme in the west, Vidzeme in the north and Latgale in the east. She's affectionately known as "Milda", which was the most popular girl's name in interwar Latvia. Given its political connotations it really is amazing that the Soviet authorities made no attempt to demolish it; perhaps they simply thought better of it.

On most days Milda is guarded by two soldiers of the Latvian Armed Forces. I sat myself down on a shaded park bench at the edge of the plaza and watched as a tourist slowly approached with camera in hand, no doubt with heady hopes of taking a photo with these two motionless specimens. She had got within only a couple of metres or so when a shout rang out, not from the soldiers but from a scary-looking man in combat fatigues whom I hadn't seen, standing at the other side of the square. "No" was the apparent message. The hapless tourist quickly scurried off, photographically none the richer.

Shortly afterward I found myself sitting in a local fast-food joint called Hesburger, which to all intents and purposes was identical to one of its more famous American cousins. To be honest I didn't really care; I was hungry and desperate for an unhealthy dose of saturated fats. I'd also decided that I didn't want to stay in Friendly Fun Franks for the entire time I would be in Riga, so I sent off a few couchsurfing requests and hoped for the best.

I was scheduled to meet Edgars at 10:00 a.m. in a café not too far from the hostel. Perhaps it was this close proximity that lulled me into a false sense of security, or perhaps I just woke up late; whatever the reason, it was already a few minutes past the hour when I finally found the place. He was already sitting there, calmly sipping a cappuccino at a table for two near the back. I rushed over to apologise but he held up his hand as if to say "Don't worry, I've only arrived myself."

I ordered a drink and then took my place opposite him in the empty seat. Edgars was a smartly dressed man with neatly cropped hair, possibly a little younger than me and who exuded a quiet confidence. I was pleased to meet him; as an assistant to a local politician in the Saeima this was a man who might be able to give me the inside track on the machinations of Riga's political elite. I wasn't going in blind, as I'd already had a hint as to his own take on the national question; we'd been chatting online in the weeks preceding my visit and he'd recently changed his profile picture to one with a small *x* made with the colours of the Latvian flag in one corner. He explained that it concerned a recent vote that had been held to decide whether Russian should join Latvian as an official language of the country. The symbol in his photograph meant that Edgars was opposed, and shortly before I visited Latvia the motion was indeed unsuccessful. "This was fortunate," said Edgars. "If it had been successful it would have meant the end of the Latvian nation."

We chatted at length, our conversation meandering through a potted history of Latvia's recent past and of its fraught relationship with its larger neighbour. I heard about Russia's need for external enemies in its own political discourse and the division of Latvia's media into separate and culturally opposed camps. It would seem that the consumers of each—albeit with an emphasis on those of a Slavic persuasion—dare not question the narratives they respectively buy into, a "legacy of the Soviet Union," he suggested. And Russia would never be "Western," because the battle between the two languages within the country was merely symptomatic of a wider ongoing regional confrontation between an authoritarian Eastern-style state and a democratic EU-led West. Any suggestion that the two languages should be on a par would merely be the thin end of the wedge: an excuse for Moscow to reassert its influence on its wayward offspring. "Latvians are barely a million strong," he said. "If we are not careful we could easily be diluted until there is nothing left." But it wasn't all siege mentality. "I think younger Russians are seeing their future as being within the EU. Russians were involved in the independence movement, after all."

Since the turn of the millennium, "Occupation of the Latvian Republic Day" has been an official occasion of remembrance in the country, observed annually on June 17. This marks the day in 1940 when Soviet troops entered the country and took over the mail, telephone, telegraph and broadcasting offices, in prelude to Latvia's full annexation some two months later. Interestingly, the only other country in the former Soviet Union to have a similar annual commemoration is Georgia, where "Soviet Occupation Day" was introduced as a direct response to Russian troops rolling into South Ossetia and Abkhazia during the 2008 war. Moldova—also on the receiving end of Russian firepower during the Transnistria conflict—made moves to introduce an equivalent, although this never came to fruition.

Edgars suggested that Victory Day was an attempt at identity building and cultural promotion for Latvia's Russians, and it occurred to me that Occupation Day might have a similar *raison d'être*. As I left I quietly wondered if he might concur with the sentiments expressed towards Latvia's Russian minority in the nearby Museum of Occupations.

I mulled this thought over as I made my way to Dzirnavu Iela, beyond the Old Town and into a mesh of dusty nineteenth- and twentieth-century city streets. The sun of the previous few days had disappeared behind a pall of grey threatening clouds that looked as if they'd burst into rain at any moment, so it was with some relief that I managed to find the place I was looking for, tucked away in a small courtyard just off the main road. I was worried that I might not find it, but I needn't have worried, for a constant stream of people was flowing in and out of an otherwise nondescript building. As I approached, an old lady stopped to ask me something. I think it was in Russian.

I joined the throng of people and was steadily propelled up a flight of stairs and into a large office that was largely bare except for a couple of tables that had been pushed together. At these the visitors were showing passports and signing what looked like some sort of petition. When it was my turn I approached one of the men seated at the desks and attempted to explain my reason for being there, but I was cut short: "You're here to meet Alise? Just a moment, please."

Alise was my next contact, a member of Latvia's Russian-speaking minority who looked even younger than Edgars and who, like him, was active in Riga's political scene. She appeared from a side room and shook my hand warmly. "Shall we go elsewhere?" she asked loudly above the din. I signalled my agreement.

We ensconced ourselves in a nearby café—the second of the day no less, and it wasn't even lunchtime yet—where Alise explained what I'd just witnessed. "We're collecting signatures as part of our campaign to force a referendum on alien citizens" she said, stirring a couple of sugars into pure-black coffee. "You'd be surprised," she continued, when I asked about the support for such a move from local Russian speakers. "Many are opposed, since they like travelling to Russia without the need for a visa."

Alise was a petite woman with strong Russian looks and long straight hair. It was clear from the outset that she possessed both a keen intellect and a sharply articulate manner. The treatment of aliens enraged her, and she spoke at great length on the injustices meted out on them: "There are 300,000 in Latvia, and it's not just travel that they face restrictions on. It's difficult for them to find jobs, vote, get good housing—all the things that normal citizens expect. And most of them have been here their entire lives. How is that fair?"

She was working for the PCTVL (Par Cilvēka Tiesībām Vienotā Latvijā) or "For Human Rights in United Latvia," which is one of two parties in Latvia to be mainly supported by ethnic Russians; the other is Saskaņas Centrs (Harmony Centre). Some—including Edgar's very own Unity Party—perceive these to be linked to the likes of Vladimir Putin's United Russia, which was a suggestion that Alise vehemently denied. Russia was not trying to influence Latvian politics; Russian speakers like her did not want to be in Russia, but instead wanted equality in an independent Latvia. But wasn't it Putin himself, I contested, who famously suggested that the dissolution of the Soviet Union was a "geopolitical disaster" that had left millions of patriotic Russians outside the nation's borders? No, said Alise, shaking her head; this has nothing to do with the issue of Russian speakers in the Baltics. Indeed, the fact that the language referendum fell victim to a slick and well-funded "No" campaign was in fact evidence of a *lack* of interference from Moscow. She went on, alleging that the incumbent government was using the issue of Russian speakers as a scapegoat to distract attention from domestic economic problems. And any problems that the Latvian language faced were not from the speaking of Russian but rather by the mass emigration of Latvians to other parts of the European Union.

"And they—the establishment—they want our petition to fail, because if we're successful it'll mean a whole new political landscape in Latvia. They won't be able to ignore us any longer, or deny us our rights. And that's why"—here she paused for just a fraction of a second—"I don't think it'll be successful. But it will help us make our point and perhaps will bring attention to our cause."

As I gathered my things I asked her where she saw her future. "Oh, I know what I'll be doing," she smiled. "I'm going to Saint Petersburg to complete my PhD. But I will return to Latvia; it's my home. Here," she said. "I have something for you." She rummaged through a satchel-like bag she had brought with her and produced a couple of slim booklets. "You might find these useful."

It had been an interesting morning. I'd spoken to two young Latvians at opposite ends of the political debate, both suspicious of the other's intentions and yet forced by the vagaries of history to call the same space home. I could see merit in both positions; Edgars's fears were grounded in the memories of 1940, of a campaign of Russification in the second half of the twentieth century and of more recent interventions by Russian forces elsewhere in the former Soviet Union; indeed, it seemed inevitable that the Kremlin would take an interest in those countries that were formerly in its orbit and that had sizable populations of ethnic Russians. Alise, on the other hand, had the persuasive argument of equality on her side; it seemed outrageous that individuals could be deprived of their civic rights through no fault of their own. And yet I could imagine such an idea of language proficiency-based citizenship appealing to the likes of the anti-immigrant brigade at home.

I went back to Franks and drank tea and cooked myself up a distinctly un-Latvian meal of pasta and pesto. Hardly anyone else was around; Viktorija had said it was still out-of-season: "Just wait a couple of weeks, you will see." So I spent the afternoon on my own, wandering around town for a short while before a brief spell of rain forced me to take cover inside a nondescript shopping centre.

I had sorted myself another couchsurf for the evening, with a young woman by the name of Kristīne; as nice as it was staying in the hostel I was still on a budget and besides, I wanted to meet more locals. We'd arranged to meet outside the train station in the early evening, which left me just enough time to stock up on provisions at the local supermarket.

I arrived at the station a little before seven. Outside the main terminal building was a small exhibition of travel photos, so I amused myself for a time imagining that I was sunning myself in front of the Great Pyramids, or taking in the views at Machu Picchu.

Suddenly my phone vibrated in my pocket. *Sorry am late, be fifteen minutes.* I sat myself down and watched the ebb and flow of people in the square. A young boy, perhaps only five or six, quickly caught my eye; he was playing some sort of game with a Frisbee that seemed to consist of flinging it as hard as he could in a random direction without thought for who might be in the way. I muttered something under my breath: probably one of those comments you find yourself making more and more often as you lose the naivety of youth and embrace the cynicism of your later years. The group of adults he was with—I couldn't tell which were the parents—were sitting drinking beer on one of the benches. Occasionally one of them would shout encouragement to the child. And of course I could see it happening almost as soon as I'd noticed them, and predictably it did indeed come to be: the disc hit me straight in the head. No apology, of course. The little darling.

Eventually I saw a person a little way off who looked like the Kristīne I'd seen online. I waved but she didn't see me; instead she reached into her bag for her phone. Mine started to ring.

"Um, hello? Are you here?" came the slightly hesitant voice.

"Yes, I'm here, I can see you. Just to your left. Yes, that's it; I'm waving! Hello!"

"Um…okay. I see you."

I noticed she wasn't really smiling which worried me a little, but as I got closer I could see that she didn't look angry or unfriendly—just completely confused.

"Hello," I said, extending a hand. "I'm Keith."

"Hi," she said, slowly shaking my hand in return. "I, um, I thought you would be a girl."

Now it was my turn to look confused.

"Your name, it's Kate, right? That's a girl's name?" She said this as if the point was a perfectly reasonable one to make.

Now it transpires that in many countries in Eastern Europe there is no equivalent to that made by the English "th" sound—Kristīne had made the assumption that the "h" was silent, that my name was pronounced "Kate," and that I must therefore be female.

"Didn't you look at my pictures on the website?" I asked. "I don't think I look much like a girl on there. I mean, is it okay? Will it be a problem?"

I'd been hanging around for almost an hour by this point and the thought of losing my place for the night had about as much appeal as playing dodge the disc with an annoying six-year-old.

"No, of course, it's fine. It's nice to meet you. Come on, let's go. And by the way"—now she gave me a little smile—"I'm Kristīne."

Kristīne's place was about a twenty-minute walk away, and as we ambled along we made small talk about her work (office administrative assistant; she'd had to stay late that evening) and mine (also a poorly paid office monkey). She seemed warm and funny and friendly and ever so slightly scatty. It was just what I needed.

It transpired that her place was on a busy road leading in a straight line from the station and very easy to find. We peeled off into a small car park and up some decrepit stairs to the first floor, replete with traces of Cyrillic on the walls. "And here is my place."

She unlocked a sturdy metal door which opened into a communal corridor. "The guy in the end flat is a bit strange," she whispered conspiratorially, "but he is harmless." Her door was equally solid-looking, and after a few twists of the key we were in.

The flat was Spartan in the extreme, basically a single room with a small kitchen area at one end. In one corner a white rabbit sat a little forlornly in a cage, and scruffy-looking coloured silhouettes of butterflies were painted on the walls. And I couldn't help noticing that there was only one bed—a double—that took up almost the entire floor space.

"Yes," said Kristīne, as if to acknowledge these observations, "I have just moved in; I admit it needs a little work, but it's alright." This turned out to be a bit of an understatement; there was no hot water and the toilet was situated behind a lockable door in the stairwell, shared as it was with the rest of the floor's inhabitants.

It also transpired that the flat had once been a tanning salon, which explained the unconventional wall art and some of the other suspect-looking marks on the walls. Kristīne explained how her parents had just bought her the place, that it had cost next to nothing, and that she'd only taken up residence a week or two previously. Apparently they were going to start renovating it soon.

"So," I said, trying not to sound too hopeful. "Where will I be sleeping?"

"Oh, in the bed, of course"—she looked at me like this was a stupid question—"I'm not staying here; I don't really like it. Especially since I cannot have a shower. So I'm going to stay at my friend's place tonight. But don't worry"—she must have caught the forlorn look that I was trying to fight away from my face—"you won't be alone. My sister's ex is staying here for a couple of days. Personally I think he's really annoying, but I've told him he has to leave by the end of the week. Well, I hope you guys will get along. His name is Eric, by the way."

This was all a bit strange, but by this point I was feeling pretty tired; it didn't look like I had much choice in the matter anyway. Kristīne showed me a secret hiding place where I could stash the keys and we agreed on a place to meet up the next day. And with that she was gone.

I consoled myself by munching on some broken biscuits that I'd found lurking at the bottom of my bag and then flicked through the booklets Alise had given me earlier that morning.

Both were concerned with the alien issue in Latvia and made for depressing reading. According to one, "noncitizens," as they are defined in a judgement handed out in the Constitutional Court of Latvia, constitute 14 per cent of the country's population and 35 per cent of what it terms the "ethnic-minority" population. Back in the 1980s, I learned, the leaders of Latvia's independence movement promised citizenship to every permanent resident who wished to be a full Latvian citizen, but barely a month after Latvia's recognition by the international community the Supreme Council began to initiate the process that would bar so many from becoming full citizens of their new state.

The Latvian authorities, as do their Estonian counterparts, take the position that while the Soviet Union had control over their territory their incorporation into the USSR was never legal. When those countries came into existence once more they saw themselves as simply a continuation of the states that had ceased to exist in 1940, rather than as brand-new nations. Citizenship, therefore, could not be automatically conferred to those who had come during the Soviet period, because they had settled under what the independent authorities considered to be an occupying power.

The other book was a collection of testimonials from alien and former alien citizens. Many expressed their frustration at a situation which they did not see as being of their own making; one man spoke of the humiliation at having to take the naturalisation test, while one woman was prevented from travelling because she was unable to replace her Soviet passport after that country had ceased to exist. Interestingly some had been born in Latvia, but others had been assigned to the region by the Soviet state— whether this was a policy of the deliberate Russification that Edgars had spoken about or simply moving resources (in this case manpower, skills and expertise) to where they were needed wasn't discussed. This was of course a political publication, but the individual stories provided a fascinating and humanising personal perspective on the impact of Latvia's citizenship laws.

Yet there was also talk of neo-Nazis and antifascists operating openly in present-day Latvia. Now while it's undoubtedly true that some extreme nationalists do exist— the annual festivities at the Freedom Monument sprang to mind—this sounded like an emotive Putin-style exaggeration. Is it really conceivable that bands of Nazis roam freely throughout the Baltics in the twenty-first century, just as Einsatzgruppen units did in 1941?

The answer, of course, is an emphatic "No." For a long time now I've been of the opinion that language like this belittles the horrific experiences of those who lived and died during the Nazi terror of the 1930s and 1940s. It also has the counterproductive result of undermining the credibility of the actual point being made, no matter how sincere or legitimate the argument might be. It's a feeling I've always had whenever comparisons are made to Hitler and his party, which as the famous Godwin's Law suggests—"As an online discussion grows longer, the probability of a comparison involving Nazis or Hitler approaches one"—happens very, very often.

I remember once standing at the Free Derry Corner memorial in Derry/Londonderry (even the name is a bone of contention among Northern Ireland's two main communities) and amongst the various inscriptions I saw references to the "Newbridge Concentration Camp," actually an internment camp in the newly created Irish Free State where antitreaty IRA members went on hunger strike in 1923. Were conditions, as the memorial implied, really on a par with the likes of Auschwitz and Buchenwald?

The meaning of the term "concentration camp" has, of course, changed over the years. Some have claimed that such camps were a British invention, coming into use at the dawn of the twentieth century to intern the families of enemy combatants and others during the Second Boer War. Indeed, conditions in the camps became increasingly harsh; thousands died as a result of their incarceration as overcrowding, neglect, poor hygiene and bad sanitation all took their toll. Yet it's also true that this was no deliberate attempt at extermination but rather a deadly combination of an incompetent administration and a distinct lack of forward planning. For conditions were harsh for the British, too; more soldiers died from disease than from actual fighting, and fatalities on both sides frequently stemmed from the scorched-earth policies that aimed to flush the Boer insurgents from their hiding places and render their guerrilla tactics unsustainable. It also had the effect of destroying most of the supplies that would have been required to sustain the ever-swelling number of refugees and inmates who flooded the camps, the law of unintended consequences proving itself with devastating consequences.

Yet such camps were nothing new. The Spanish had similar arrangements in force in Cuba during the Ten Years' War of 1868–78, as did the United States in the Philippines at the same time as the British campaign in South Africa. It was only with the Nazis' introduction of deliberate and systematic mass murder on an industrial scale that the term "concentration camp"—originally intended to refer to any compound given over to the forced detention of a group of individuals—developed the dubious and deadly connotations that we associate with the term today.

Of course all this is little consolation to those who lost their lives, but the German association with the concentration camp is now so complete that the mere mention of the phrase conjures up appalling images of emaciated shaven-headed inmates, gas chambers and crematoria. Could it be that those trying to promote their own narrative might attempt to use this confusion to subliminally suggest that their own experiences were on the same level as the utter evil that was the Holocaust, no matter how ridiculous or potentially offensive such an approach is? Or am I simply being cynical?

I was making my way along a quiet street somewhere near the Latvian Academy of Sciences, the large Stalinist construction that looms over this part of the city. Its grandiose classical style bears a striking resemblance to other buildings found throughout the former Eastern Bloc, and the more observant may realise that this is no coincidence: together it was intended that the buildings would collectively serve to extol the eternal victory of the socialist cause. Most of them—the so-called Seven Sisters—are in Moscow, and the others can be found in Kiev, Bucharest, Prague and Warsaw. Needless to say opinions about the buildings are polarised, with many resentful at these concrete testaments to Soviet domination. I personally rather like their over-the-top style, but then there's no accounting for taste.

I was not alone, for Kristīne was with me and together we were making our way to a friend's house for what I had been reliably assured would be a "good party." It had already been an enjoyable day, the highlight of which had been a trip around the city's beautiful Art Nouveau district with Kristīne and a shy-but-friendly chap by the name of Janis. It was obvious that Janis had romantic intentions towards my host but the feeling didn't appear to be reciprocated, as Kristīne was at pains to point out— several times, in fact—when he was safely out of earshot. I wasn't entirely convinced by her protestations but I didn't really mind playing the third wheel, and at the end of our walk we rewarded ourselves by spending a pleasant hour or two sipping beers by the Daugava and dodging the police car that would swing by occasionally to make sure we weren't breaking the city's strict al fresco drinking laws. To my somewhat considerable relief Eric had also turned out to be a nice guy and not at all annoying, and we'd spent the night before chatting about this and that. "So nothing happened, then," Kristīne teased me with a wink. I refused to dignify her question with an answer, which caused her great amusement.

Tonight it was someone's birthday—a twenty-second, I think—and after flashbacks of Ambla had threatened to ruin the evening I'd been assured that this time I was definitely invited. The place was a big shared house, and by the sound of the music carried on the evening breeze it was clear that proceedings were already in full swing by the time we knocked on the big black door. It was opened by a tall man who gave Kristīne a big hug and me an equally warm handshake when we were introduced.

Inside were lots of people doing all the sorts of things that you might expect at a party—eating, drinking, listening to dodgy records from the 1980s and generally making merry. Kristīne disappeared somewhere, while I fell in with a group of young Latvians playing a nameless card game whose rules I couldn't quite get to grips with and which of course was all the more fun as a result.

Our conversation meandered through an entire spectrum of unlikely subjects, from Latvia's chances in the upcoming Eurovision song contest (very good, I was told) to the relative merits of Riga's black balsam, the dark and sticky local liqueur that tastes a bit like cough medicine—appropriate, perhaps, given that it was originally marketed as a health tonic. I got to sample a few drops of the stuff and the powerful, rich flavour really was enough to put hairs on your chest.

When the reason for my visit to Riga soon became apparent the talk quickly turned to Victory Day and, by extension, the people who chose to attend it. I was surprised to find that views were uniformly uncompromising; one person suggested that the whole concept of the day was to be deliberately confrontational and provocative, and had the recent efforts to make Russian an official language succeeded it would have resulted in the almost-certain death of the Latvian language. Another said that she would only shop at Latvian-owned stalls in the local market, and if they dared greet her in Russian she would simply take her custom elsewhere.

Katya, the birthday girl, took a seat in the small circle of friends and prised open a small album that she had been clutching in her arms. In it were photos of friends from previous gatherings, and as she flicked through the pages I recognised some of the partygoers from that evening's soirée. The picture that caught my eye showed them all dressed up in cheap tracksuits, tacky and overly ostentatious jewellery, and with copious layers of fake tan. "It's a Russian party," she giggled. "We're all dressed up like the Russians do."

Katya and her peers were university students, all born after independence and all native Latvian speakers. I wondered how much interaction they'd had with Russian speakers of a similar age, and if they would actually find that—language barrier aside—they would have more in common than they might actually think. Or perhaps not. I really didn't know.

And I wondered if Kersti and Jaan, sitting with their black-and-white cat in the glow of a Tartu evening, would have much to say about their choice of party outfits.

Riga, as befits any national capital, has a few interesting museums and I whiled away a couple of pleasant days shuffling between them. The Museum of Medical History, barely a stone's throw from the Freedom Monument, was wonderfully quirky, with lifelike exhibits illustrating humanity's first tentative forays into medical care—the trepanning of an unfortunate native with a sharp stick and an amputation with only prayer as an anaesthetic was enough to convince me that contemporary health care was somewhat preferable to that practised in days gone by. Perhaps most disturbing, however, was the stuffed remains of a two-headed dog that had been created Frankenstein-style by Soviet scientists by grafting the head and front legs of a small dog onto the back of a larger one. Reportedly the poor thing(s?) lived for several days after the procedure and grainy video footage of their handiwork can easily be found on the internet.

The Latvian War Museum was also worthwhile, and not simply because entry was free. Partly housed in the impressive medieval Powder Tower, it covered a range of subjects that was now becoming increasingly familiar; the establishment of the state and the interwar period, then the war of attrition against the invading Nazis and Soviets. The attendants also had that delightfully irritating Eastern European habit of following you around as you walk from room to room examining the exhibits, like some sort of ever-suspicious curatorial chaperones ready to beat you over the head should you look like you might even sneeze on a display case.

Perhaps most moving, though, were photographs of cheery-looking Forest Brothers juxtaposed with Soviet Intelligence pictures of summarily executed partisans, their bodies dumped in public as a warning to any others who might be tempted to take up the cause. Who knows, it might even have been the same individuals in both.

I ended my first visit to Riga where I'd started—in Friendly Fun Franks, sipping a beer and chatting to Liga. We'd been talking about where I might head next—perhaps to the coast or to the rural hinterland. "Daugavpils," I said. "That's where I'm headed. Daugavpils."

"Daugavpils" she frowned, with a mixture of bemusement and thinly disguised contempt. "Daugavpils is a… Russian city."

CHAPTER 7

Surfing the Couch

∗ ∗ ∗

MY FIRST EVER COUCHSURFING EXPERIENCE was in Helsinki. I'd had a bit of trouble finding a place to stay but I eventually managed to get an offer from a guy called Ilari, who for the sake of convenience promised to meet me in the centre of town. I had to admit that I was a little nervous about the whole affair; I still wasn't convinced that this couchsurfing thing was completely legit, and by the time I rolled into the Finnish capital it was well past midnight and I was feeling extremely tired from the day's travels. Waiting for me was my host—a huge shaven-headed hulk of a man, well over six feet tall and broad enough to give an oak tree a run for its money. We boarded a bus and headed out to the suburbs, Ilari's warm handshake only slightly helping to quell my growing feeling of unease—after all, I had no idea where exactly we were headed or what would happen when we got there. Visions of newspapers with headlines describing the disappearance and brutal murder of a hapless British tourist filled my mind, and as we climbed the stairs to his apartment in the thick black of night I couldn't help but wonder if Helsinki would be both the start and end of my Baltic odyssey.

As it transpired, my fears couldn't have been more misplaced. Ilari was utterly charming, and we chatted deep into the early hours about travel and work and of life itself. It turned out that he'd spent time in Yemen as a security guard, a posting that had been particularly challenging given his pale Nordic complexion: "I used to get through a bottle of sun cream a week," he mused. And when I asked him what his motivation was for hosting strangers his answer was wonderfully poetic: "Ah, it's simple. At the moment I'm unable to travel, so in this way the world can come to me instead."

We spent the next day taking in the sights of the city, from elegant churches and squares to my personal favourite, the beautiful art-deco Central Railway Station: I particularly liked the colossal muscle-bound statues clutching globe-shaped lamps flanking both sides of the main entrance. Finland, of course, was also once part of the Russian Empire and surprisingly a statue of Tsar Alexander II still stands proud outside the Lutheran Cathedral. It might seem a little strange to see a monument to former Russian domination in this, the most northerly national capital in the European Union. But Alexander is widely credited with promoting Finnish autonomy by reconvening the Diet of Finland in 1863, establishing Finland's own currency (the *markka*, since replaced by the euro) and the first railways,

by encouraging foreign investment and industrial development, and elevating Finnish to that of a national language.
Alexander himself was assassinated in Saint Petersburg in
1881, the victim of an anarchist's bomb, but to this day he's
still remembered in Finland as "The Good Tsar."

Finland had found itself in a difficult position at the
end of the Second World War. Previously allied with
Nazi Germany, the country had to do some nifty diplomatic manoeuvring to avoid complete absorption into the
new Soviet sphere of influence rapidly being created in
Eastern Europe. In return for the retention of democracy
and parliamentarianism, successive Finnish governments
followed a doctrine of cordial relations with the USSR at a
time when the iron curtain was very much becoming both
an ideological and physical barrier across the continent;
indeed, Finland signed an "Agreement of Friendship,
Cooperation, and Mutual Assistance" with the Soviet
Union in 1948—a country it had been at war with just
a few years earlier. Under the terms of this pact Finland
was able to adopt a policy of "active neutrality," retaining
its independence while maintaining extensive trade links
both with capitalist nations and those of the Warsaw Pact.
The idea was simple, if tricky: to fend off Soviet interference by playing down relations with the West.

This process, by which one powerful country influ-
ences the policies of a smaller neighbouring state, has since
become known as "Finlandisation." The term, originating in West German political debates in the 1960s and

1970s, is not intended as a compliment; it suggests a fawn-
ing and excessive adaption meant to appease a much larger
neighbouring power. In Finland this manifested itself in
a number of ways, including self-censorship of the media
and the proscription of films and books considered to be
anti-Soviet in tone. One of the most famous examples was
the banning of the 1970 film version of *One Day in the Life
of Ivan Denisovich* by Finnish director Caspar Wrede; its
story of a routine day in the life of an inmate in a Soviet
gulag too much for domestic legislators nervous at damag-
ing the Finnish-Soviet relationship.

I was considering all of this as my train rumbled slowly
across the Latvian countryside, through a now-familiar
landscape of wide-open pastures and pine forests. The
sun that had accompanied me during my stay in Riga had
gone, replaced with dark menacing clouds of the like not
seen since Narva.

I'd arranged a place to stay with a young chap called
Vladislav, who—as his name suggested—spoke Russian as
his first language. We'd exchanged a couple of messages
and he had very kindly agreed to meet me at the station.
And, as I disembarked onto the platform, I caught sight of
a man holding a piece of paper with both my name and,
inexplicably, a picture of a bicycle on it. The only problem
was that the man was quite clearly not Vladislav.

"Oh hello, it's Keith?" the man asked as I approached
him. I nodded in confirmation, and he proffered a hand
in greeting in return. "I'm Sergei, I work with Vlad. He

is, uh, having problem with his girlfriend, so he ask me to meet you here. We go to him now."

Sergei seemed friendly enough, so I let him lead the way down Daugavpils's long main street, unsure what to expect from a city that I'd heard so many negative things about. Yet despite the warnings first impressions were, on the surface, reasonably favourable; the streets were well kept and the buildings that lined them tidy and well maintained. Sergei himself was big—not on an Ilari scale, but getting there—and probably in his mid-twenties or thereabouts. He was dark-haired and wore glasses that set off overly stubble-rimmed cheeks, and my initial reservations quickly evaporated as he chatted in a hesitant English that conveyed a real warmth. He seemed genuinely pleased to have been given the task of meeting and greeting a random Brit while the original host was experiencing some kind of domestic crisis.

"I have to ask you," I said after a while. "I really liked having my name held on a piece of paper like that; I mean, it's the first time I've ever had someone holding out my name and I've always wanted someone to. But I mean, what's with the picture of the bicycle?"

"Yes, it is strange, I agree. I not really sure. Vlad said you would have bicycle with you."

We eventually caught up with Vlad at his apartment, another Khrushchyovka located in an unremarkable Daugavpils suburb. Sergei and I had taken a bus to get there via a jungle of towering and seemingly identical apartment blocks of various colours and hues, all with that same basic bland design. "Yes, even I have trouble remembering which one it is," my companion confided guiltily as we reached what was the right street. In fact Sergei's concerns were so genuine that he had to phone Vlad to find out exactly which apartment was his, and shortly afterward we were hammering on a heavy red metal door. It opened to reveal the Vlad I recognised from the pictures online. "Welcome!" he beamed, stepping aside to let me through. A few words of Russian were exchanged with my minder, and with that Sergei waved his goodbyes.

Vlad's apartment was surprisingly spacious, decorated in a slightly dated but nonetheless extremely comfortable wooden-panel interior that at some point had clearly had quite a lot of money spent on it.

"Oh," he chuckled as he saw my eyes wander around the decor. "It used to be my parents' place. I don't really like it but it's okay for now. Here, this is where you'll be sleeping, it should be comfortable for your stay, I hope. Do you need a towel?"

I liked Vlad. He had a warm laugh and a scruffy mop of hair framed by what I suspected was an unintentionally but nonetheless rather trendy pair of black-rimmed glasses. He was, I supposed, about the

Keith Ruffles

The deserted corridors of Tallinn's Patarei Prison

The author with the Bronze Soldier of Tallinn.

Soviet Man in Sillamae, Estonia

The Latvian Riflemen stand proud in Riga's Old Town

Checking out the displays during Riga's
Victory Day celebrations

Abandoned Communist Party Headquarters
in Daugavpils, Latvia

Lenin entertains visitors in Grutas Park, Lithuania

The names of the killed adorn the walls of the
Lithuanian Genocide Museum in Vilnius

A peaceful scene somewhere in Lithuania

same age as me, and as we sat in his kitchen sipping black tea—with not a drop of milk in sight but as much lemon as we could hope for—we chatted in the format that was by now starting to become familiar as a regular couch-surfer: I was his first guest and I was on a trip around the Baltics; he'd just returned from a cycling trip in Vietnam with his boss (apparently the relationship had deteriorated somewhat over a broken pannier); he was looking forward to welcoming people from other parts of the world to Daugavpils. It also transpired that the bicycle reference that had so stumped Sergei and me was actually meant for another couchsurfer, scheduled to arrive the following week.

"And I have to ask," I ventured. "I hope everything is okay with the girlfriend? I mean, is it anything to do with me staying here?"

"Well…yes, it is, sort of. But please, don't worry. She is not a very adventurous person. We are always fighting over silly things. Well, there is one reason. She is from Ukraine."

My main reason for visiting Daugavpils, other than to sample the atmosphere of Latvia's most Russian city, was to visit the huge citadel that lies about a mile or so from the centre of town. Vlad and I caught the bus early in the morning, our English conversation attracting the glances of a few of our fellow commuters. We parted company outside his office—he divulged that he was a computer programmer of some sorts but I failed to fully comprehend his techno-babble—and we agreed to meet back there at 5:00 p.m. or thereabouts when he finished.

I marched off confidently in the direction of the citadel. It was another overcast day, humid even, and as I strolled along an incongruous street that my map assured me was the right direction I could even feel a little bit of rain. Why was it, I mused, that the only times I ever experienced bad weather in the Baltics was whenever I was close to the Russian border?

After half an hour or so I'd left the city behind, and just when I thought that perhaps I'd taken a wrong turn I found, just beyond where the road ducked under a railway bridge, the entrance to the citadel—a squat, solid gate of yellow stone flanked by the remains of walls, ditches and other similarly impressive and impregnable fortifications.

Daugavpils's fortress, occupying a strategic position overlooking the Daugava River, was originally built by the Tsarist authorities in the latter half of the eighteenth century, only to be thoroughly dismantled by Napoleon's armies during the campaign of 1812. Most of what can be seen today dates from the last couple of centuries, and for many years it served as a Soviet aviation-training school right up until Latvian independence. The whole complex is now a curious mixture of the post-apocalyptic and the urbane: abandoned military buildings stand decaying and crumbling in the damp Baltic air, while residents of the Khrushchyovka-style barracks that would have once housed the heroic airmen of tomorrow continue to eke out a living.

I spent a couple of hours wandering around the streets, many of which were in the process of being dug up and re-laid in a massive renovation exercise. Lumps of rubble and brick were strewn everywhere which made the going difficult, but the unremitting bleakness was livened up by the odd tree and period artillery piece; the latter probably dated from before the Russian Revolution.

At the centre of the citadel's grounds a small square-shaped park offered a splash of greenery and a respite from the drabness, but beyond this the apartments and the people and the activity stopped completely; the farther I went, the further it felt from civilisation. I crept inside one abandoned building, lured into the blackness by an overgrown doorway with its door long since gone. Heart pounding in my ears, I'd barely gone farther than a few feet in the inky darkness when I heard a menacing growl, the padding of feet and a series of ominously angry barks that grew steadily louder. I began to back away before the flight instinct took over, suddenly terrified at the prospect of being eaten alive by some unspeakable canine monstrosity. And it was just as well, for as I stumbled back into the street a giant Alsatian burst into view, all bared teeth and snarling lips, seemingly ready to pounce before defiantly standing its ground as if to warn me not to even think about coming any closer. Deciding that discretion was most definitely the better part of valour I chose to go the long way around instead.

At the very back of the fortress, which was by now thankfully dog-free, I came across one dilapidated building with faint white Cyrillic letters still legible across its shell: "KPSS," the Russian initials of the Communist Party of the Soviet Union. Inside I found eerily empty rooms filled with random detritus: chairs and desks and other bits of furniture, all left to rot. Cobwebs and dust hung heavy in the air, and only the unsteady, rickety rotten wooden floorboards prevented me from exploring any further. To the wry observer the melancholy state of the place would have been a fitting metaphor for the USSR's demise.

It might seem strange, then, that around a thousand people still live in the fortress, trapped in their apartments as the rest of the citadel crumbles around them. Many of them once would have been employed in the aviation school; they simply refused to budge once it shut down and the local authorities were more than happy to oblige; rehousing such a large number of people during economically straitened times would have presented an almost insurmountable problem. The residents of this strange little self-contained community paid me little heed as I poked and pried and occasionally beat a hasty retreat around their unusual home.

The fortress had one more surprise in store before I left. Tucked out of the way was a fully restored building, much smaller than the others, and one that might have once been a chapel or some such. Inside were several displays documenting the fortress's colourful life. A young man quickly rose from behind a desk as I entered, eager to engage his latest visitor. His English was excellent, and we spoke about the grand vision that was being planned for the citadel that, he said, would see it transform into *the* major tourist attraction of eastern Latvia, perhaps of the entire Baltics. He must have caught my expression, because he nodded in acknowledgement. "Yes, it's unlikely I know when you see the state of the place," he said wistfully, "but we're hoping that with European Union money we might succeed. We can hope."

I didn't want to say anything to discourage this vision but I hated to think how long it would take to finish rebuilding everything, because there didn't seem to be much work going on while I was there. It suddenly occurred to me that I hadn't seen a single worker or labourer the entire time I'd been on site despite it being a standard—if slightly wet—weekday afternoon, and to describe the task as a monumental one would be a real study in understatement. It also made me wonder if Riga might ever be tempted to overlook investment opportunities in this, its most Russian and most wayward region. It did seem a shame, though, for whilst I doubted that Daugavpils would ever become the Latvian equivalent of the Tower of London or the Kremlin a lot of work was clearly needed just to prevent the place from collapsing in on itself. And this wasn't just some monument in need of preservation; this was a living, working home that desperately needed new life breathed into it.

And as I bade the man farewell I hit on another truth: perhaps I should have got that rabies vaccination after all.

Around one hundred thousand people live in Daugavpils. The name literally means "Daugava Castle" and it sits snugly in Latvia's south-eastern corner, miles or so from Riga and only twenty miles from the borders with Lithuania and Belarus. The town's history came into being in 1275 when the Livonian order built Dünaburg Castle a short distance up the Daugava River, and after a few centuries had passed it became a part of the Polish-Lithuanian Commonwealth. Things stayed that way until its gradual absorption into the expanding Russian Empire towards the end of the eighteenth century. Now known as *Dvinsk*, the settlement continued to grow and prosper and it rapidly became a thriving centre of Jewish culture; according to the census of 1897 there were 32,400 Jews out of a total figure of just under 70,000: some 44 per cent of the population. The celebrated Russian photographer Sergey Prokudin-Gorsky visited the town on the eve of the First World War, his marvellous colour images depicting a neat town of churches, red-brick buildings and tree-lined avenues. After the city's successful capture by a combined Polish-Latvian force in December 1919, upon independence the new authorities in Riga gave the town its current name.

Daugavpils's border location has given it something of a Wild West—or in this case Wild East—reputation as a hotbed of organised crime, a status no doubt bolstered by the murder of Deputy Mayor Grigorijs Ņemcovs in broad daylight in 2010. Founder of *Million*, the largest Russian-language regional newspaper in Latvia, the publication prided itself in uncovering local government corruption and mismanagement—subjects that likely earned Ņemcovs many enemies. No one has ever been prosecuted for the crime.

Ņemcovs also founded the civic-society movement Latgales Tauta—the Nation of Latgale. Latgale is the easternmost of Latvia's regions, and it's not just language that sets it apart from the rest of the country; whilst most of Latvia is Lutheran it is Roman Catholicism that predominates here, and the most important Catholic shrine in the country is found in the small town of Aglona, some thirty miles or so from Daugavpils. Latgale—named after one of the original Baltic tribes that settled in the region some four thousand years ago—has a much stronger regional identity than is found elsewhere in Latvia, and some consider the local dialect to be so distinct as to constitute a separate language. Indeed, muted campaigns have even been mounted to incorporate Latgale into Russia, with the occasional small demonstration outside the Latvian embassy in Moscow eliciting modest support. Coincidence or not, this was the only part of Latvia to oppose EU membership.

That evening I joined Vlad on a walk from his apartment. Our route took us through a nearby wooded area, a coniferous forest crisscrossed by tracks and the occasional fellow hiker. "We're going the slightly longer way," said Vlad, "but I prefer it. It's nicer than the road."

After a while we emerged onto a network of lanes, lined with the sort of small wooden houses that had proven to be so charming in Tartu. Here we were away from the apartment blocks and from Daugavpils proper; this leafy suburb felt much more like a countryside village than part of a larger urban accumulation. A blink of an eye and we were firmly in rural Latvia.

Eventually we came to a small track and stopped outside one house. "My father's place," Vlad explained as he knocked on the door. "Just be careful when we go in. He's rebuilding the place, and I think a lot of the floorboards are missing."

My immediate impression was of something resembling a building site; chipboard lined the floors, paint cans and other clutter lay festooned about the place, and I think some of the walls were missing too. But on the floor above things were different; a whole floor had been completely renovated and it looked fantastic. Given the missing walls below the fact that it had an upstairs floor felt like a considerable achievement.

Vlad's father was a kindly, portly man with a cheerful face framed by a bushy grey moustache and a broad smile.

We dined that evening on bread and sausages as we heard tales of harder times, when even basic staples such as these could be hard to find. Vlad's father—it was only afterward that I realised that I'd never learned his name—was born in modern-day Belarus; with his part-Polish ancestry, he embodied in some ways the overlapping identities of these shifting borderlands. We left feeling full and happy, having been welcomed into the simple home of a man who had completed a PhD in Saint Petersburg and had lectured at the University of Riga back in the days of the Soviet Union.

Dark clouds that had been gathering all day had gradually taken on a more menacing appearance as we wined and dined, and as we made our way home a few drops belied the downpour that was to come. Our pace quickened but it was to no avail, for as the apartment blocks loomed nearer the heavens opened in a torrent of rain and lightning. I don't know if you've ever been caught out in a thunderstorm, but it can be a surprisingly frightening and elemental experience. All sorts of scenarios ran through my head as lightning pierced the night sky, deafening our ears with every crash. What was it you were supposed to do in this situation: do I run for the nearest tree, or do I stay in the open? Am I wearing rubber-soled shoes? Will I survive a direct hit?

Vlad thought all this to be hilarious of course, and by the time we finally reached his apartment we were cold and soaked to the bone but thankfully free of electrocution. It had been a fitting end to an interesting stay in this city on the fringe of Latvian society—of Latvia itself and yet somehow a place apart. I was glad I came.

CHAPTER 8

A Stumble in the Dark

* * *

Litwo! Ojczyzno moja! ty jesteś jak zdrowie;
Ile cię trzeba cenić, ten tylko się dowie,
Kto cię stracił.

Lithuania, my country! You are as good health:
How much one should prize you, he only can tell
Who has lost you.

SO GOES THE OPENING TO the epic poem "Pan Tadeusz," by the writer and philosopher Adam Mickiewicz. It's a suitably melodramatic tale of family feuds and vengeance, thwarted love, murder, guilt, deathbed revelations and reconciliations, all set during the chaotic years of the Napoleonic Wars.

What is interesting, however, is that Pan Tadeusz, as with all of Mickiewicz's work, is written in Polish and is considered the national poem of Poland. Indeed, it's a compulsory text in Polish schools and Miciewicz is considered the first of the "Three Bards"—a triumvirate of poets who lived and worked in exile during the partitions of Poland that ended the existence of a sovereign Polish state. As the fathers of the modern Polish romantic movement in the early nineteenth century the Bards were thought to not only give voice to a growing national sentiment but also to foresee the nation's future at a time when both Poland and Lithuania were mere territories on the western fringes of the Russian Empire.

Born in Zaoise—modern-day Zavosse, in Belarus—into an upper-class Polish family in 1798, from a young age Mickiewicz became active in the nascent independence movement and spent five years in exile before escaping for good in 1829, settling first in Rome and then in Paris where Pan Tadeusz would be published. He spent much of his career writing and lecturing and welcomed any development that might weaken Russia and re-establish Poland. It was the latter that would eventually lead to his death in Istanbul, having contracted cholera during efforts to support Polish forces fighting for the Ottoman Empire in the Crimean War.

He is jointly (and exclusively) claimed by modern Poland, Lithuania and Belarus as one of their own: a suggestion Mickiewicz most likely would have rejected. When Pan Tadeusz was published in 1834 nationalism was still in a nascent state of development in a Europe dominated by just a few huge yet incredibly diverse empires. Mickiewicz's reference to "Lithuania," therefore, was both a reference to the geographic area of Greater Lithuania as well as a homage to the Polish-Lithuanian Commonwealth, which had ceased to exist upon the first partition of Poland in 1772. Back then any perceived differences between Lithuania and Poland, united by their staunch Catholicism and opposition to Russian Orthodoxy, were regarded as largely cosmetic and Mickiewicz's life embodied that union and the shifting borders that so typify the region's history.

Any such solidarity between Lithuania and Poland soon evaporated at the end of the First World War. Conflict between the two new states, which had previously found a common enemy in the Bolshevik armies, erupted as each country claimed Vilnius for its own. As the battle lines ebbed and flowed, Polish general Żeligowski marched into the city with the intention of defending "the right of self-determination of local Poles"; he proclaimed the creation of the independent Republic of Central Lithuania in October 1920. Further advances were halted by Lithuanian troops and shortly afterward a ceasefire was declared, but despite mediation by the nascent League of Nations the republic was incorporated into Poland as the Wilno Voivodeship some two years later. Lithuania, unsurprisingly, never accepted this outcome and cut off all diplomatic relations with its former ally until 1938, and even then only acquiesced to their restoration on the threat of war by a bullish Polish government. During this period the Lithuanian authorities sat in Kaunas, seething at what they saw as the theft of their rightful capital.

It's a little ironic, perhaps, that the architect of the Polish takeover of Wilno (as Vilnius was known during this period) was masterminded by one Marshall Józef Piłsudski, himself a Polish-Lithuanian born in a small village near the present-day border of Lithuania and Belarus. Piłsudski became the newly independent Poland's first chief of state and commanded the Polish forces that helped to define the country's borders. He was a firm believer in a diverse country and even had visions of resurrecting the Commonwealth; his dream of Międzymorze—the "Intermarium"—would see a federation of Central and Eastern Europe stretching from the Baltic to the Black Seas under the aegis of Poland. Lithuania and Ukraine, however, saw such plans as a threat to their independence and the proposals went nowhere.

Piłsudski eventually had to settle for a Poland that was divested of his Lithuanian homeland, but his emotional link to the region was never truly broken; upon his death in 1935 his heart was buried in Vilnius's Rasos Cemetery, near the grave of his mother. Today the site, located in a section dedicated to Polish soldiers killed in the Soviet and Lithuanian wars, is a pilgrimage spot for Polish nationalists and a considerable source of contention in this sensitive area. His star tarnished during the communist era, Piłsudski's reputation has seen something of a renaissance in the past two decades; an increasingly authoritarian form of government following a coup d'état in 1926, combined with his stringently anti-Russian views, are now seen by many as minor blemishes in the wider battle to secure Poland's independence.

Today, however, virtually no one talks of Polish-Lithuanian unification. Mickiewicz's dream of a nation independent from Russia may have been realised, but the competing aims of modern nationalism dictates that Poland and Lithuania are now separate places, distinct and apart. Relations between the two can still be strained, even in the post-Communist world; some accused the Soviet Union of attempting to use Lithuania's Polish minority to undermine the push for independence via the *Yedinstvo* ("Unity") movement during the dying days of the USSR, whilst Polish nationalists continue to press for the return of the Wilno district. The removal of border posts under the Schengen Agreement has, it seems, done little to satisfy these competing ambitions.

Yet such are the contradictions of this region that the Polish-Lithuanian connection continues to inspire pride in both nations. The Nazis and Soviets too sought to gain capital from what was, at the time of its formal creation in 1569, one of the largest and most progressive states in Europe, and no single event embodies this peculiar legacy better than the medieval Battle of Grunwald.

Grunwald was fought in the context of the wars for religious and territorial supremacy that ravaged the southern Baltic throughout the fourteenth and fifteenth centuries.

Determined to finally stamp their authority on the unruly inhabitants of the region after a series of local uprisings, in 1410 the German-Prussian Teutonic Knights were decisively defeated by an alliance of the Kingdom of Poland and the Grand Duchy of Lithuania in one of the largest and fiercest battles ever seen on the continent. For the Knights the event was catastrophic; most of their leadership was killed or taken prisoner and the battle permanently shifted the balance of power in Eastern Europe, marking the rise of the nascent Polish-Lithuanian Union as the dominant military and political force in the region.

In the centuries that followed, the battle was used to support wildly different political narratives as various nations sought to claim its legacy as their own. In Lithuania Grunwald became synonymous with the Grand Duchy's peak, inspiring national pride and resistance to the Germanisation and Russification policies of those respective empires during the Romantic era of Mickiewicz and his peers. Similarly, in Poland the portrayal of the Knights as bloodthirsty invaders who were successfully repelled by a small oppressed nation would go on to inspire the erection of a large monument in the centre of Krakow to mark the 500th anniversary of the great victory; after the memorial's destruction during the Nazi occupation it would be rebuilt by the Communist government in 1976. And the participation of three regiments from Smolensk meant that Russia—and later the Soviet Union—saw it as a pan-Slavic victory against the invading German horde, a medieval rehearsal for the Great Patriotic War; indeed, the cry of Grunwald was used to inspire the heroic defence of cities such as Stalingrad against the Nazi hordes during World War II.

Yet for Germany the Battle of Tannenberg, as the called it, carried completely different connotations. They saw the Knights as heroic and noble men who brought the twin lights of Christianity and civilisation to the East; when German forces under Paul von Hindenburg defeated the Russian Second Army in the opening salvos of the First World War not far from where the medieval battle had taken place they decided to give their victory the same name, as if to avenge the defeat of the Teutonic Knights five centuries earlier. Now located in East Prussia, that easternmost portion of Germany hived off from the rest of the country after World War I, the interwar regime subsequently built a large memorial on the site of the modern confrontation; when Hindenburg died in 1934 the Nazis interred his coffin at the memorial against his wishes. His remains were hastily removed and much of the memorial demolished as the Red Army approached in 1945; the Polish authorities took care of the rest a few years later and today very little remains.

The bus rattled its way through a verdant landscape of woodlands and lakes. The terrain was hillier here than I'd seen elsewhere in the Baltics, and I enjoyed the way the surroundings gleamed and glinted after the heavy rainfall of the past few days. I was on my way to the Lithuanian city of Kaunas, having risen at the crack of dawn to catch the first bus from Daugavpils. At the station I witnessed a sight that I would see several times during the trip; a drunk man, on this occasion sitting next to a young woman who looked to be a student or something similar. She looked increasingly uncomfortable at his clumsy attempts at conversation, desperately trying to not look up from her book as he rattled on in some unintelligible, alcohol-riddled monologue. Perhaps I should have done something to shoo him away but, like everyone else, I kept quiet. I think deep down—and to my shame—I was simply glad it wasn't me he was bothering.

The beautiful landscape was so captivating that I didn't even notice us crossing the border. We were firmly in Kresy Wschodnie now—the huge swathe of Poland that was absorbed into the USSR in September 1939, an annexation that the Allies ratified at the end of the war. The whole of Poland was effectively shifted westwards, the loss of Kresy compensated by the acquisition of large portions of German territory including half of East Prussia as well as Pomerania and Silesia. "Kresy" literally means "Borderlands," and the myth of Polish Kresy as a peaceful, idyllic rural land has captivated generations of Poles ever since its loss. Indeed, cultural affinity to the region remains strong, and towns such as Vilnius, Hrodna and Lviv—once considered thoroughly Polish— that transferred to the independent nations of Lithuania,

Belarus and Ukraine respectively upon the Soviet Union's collapse are now the focus of a particular type of Polish nostalgia. A large Polish minority still exists in Kresy and in some districts forms a majority, particularly along the border between Lithuania and Belarus. A survey in 2012 prompted over four million Polish citizens—15 per cent of Poland's population—to claim a direct family link to the region.

I could certainly concur with the argument that Kresy is indeed wonderful, and as we made our way through this gorgeous little corner of Lithuania I began to look forward to our final destination with a mounting sense of excitement. Kaunas had been the first Baltic city that I had visited back with my dad a few years before; we had arrived there almost by accident, our appearance facilitated by the vagaries of budget flights. I'd read up on the place beforehand and at first glance it seemed like one to avoid—Kaunas had developed a worrying reputation for organised crime in the chaotic first decade of independence and promised to be altogether less salubrious then its elegant cousin, the capital. Our timetable demanded that we stay for a couple of nights, and I was nervous that it might not be the best place to kick-start our holiday.

It transpired that I needn't have worried, because Kaunas really is a lovely city in which to while away some time. I'd booked my dad and I into a room in a monastic guest house of all places, slap bang in the Old Town near the confluence of the Nemunis and Neris Rivers that bequeaths the town its strategic importance. It was a Spartan but comfortable base and was of the oh-so-quirky variety that would characterise our few days in Lithuania. We enjoyed strolling its busy streets, from the cobbles of the Old Town to the café-lined Laisvės Alėja, the straight-as-an-arrow pedestrianised promenade that is said to be the longest of its kind in Eastern Europe. We visited the Devil Museum, an institution dedicated to the Satanic-themed collection of a local artist and various subsequent donations made over the years. Full of representations of Beelzebub in various forms such as masks and statues, particularly memorable was a sinister model of a demonic Hitler and Stalin dancing their murderous way across a skull-filled Lithuania. The museum wasn't merely a repository for devil-themed memorabilia, however; it also housed an impressive collection of folk art, in particular *rūpintojėlis*: intricately carved wooden statues of the "Pensive Christ," a seated and contemplative Jesus that became immensely popular in Poland and Lithuania in the late Middle Ages.

Lithuania, just like Poland, is proud of its Catholic roots, and yet perhaps the strangest thing about this contemporary strength is that Lithuania was the last nation in Europe to convert from paganism, doing so only in the fourteenth century. It's perhaps no surprise that a great deal of syncretism went on to make the religion more palatable and accessible to its new adherents, and the museum's religious images of seed sowers recalled pagan fertility symbols of an earlier period. It's just possible to glimpse this pagan past when you see modern Lithuanian girls with crowns of flowers in their hair.

Indeed, even today some would see the revival of Lithuania's pre-Christian culture as a reassertion of a more genuine Lithuanian identity. The most famous of these reassertions is the movement known as Romuva, which claims to promote the continued existence of Baltic pagan traditions including music, singing, art and the like. With its focus on Baltic culture, the Soviets not surprisingly regarded the movement as an overtly nationalist group and as such was actively suppressed during Lithuania's stint as a socialist republic. It won status as a recognised faith shortly after independence.

Still, it would be unfair to underestimate the importance of Roman Catholicism in contemporary Lithuania. As was the case in Poland, the Catholic Church became a rallying cry for those who were opposed to Communist rule; centred on the town of Šiluva, about an hour north of Kaunas and where the Virgin Mary was said to have miraculously appeared in 1608, Pope John Paul II—a Pole—visited shortly after independence to rapturous crowds. Today Šiluva continues to be a place of pilgrimage for Catholics from all over Lithuania and beyond.

But perhaps the most peculiar site in Kaunas was not to be found in the Devil Museum but in the basement of the squat Garrison Church that stands prominently in a commanding position at one end of Laisvės Alėja.

This baroque edifice, now a Roman Catholic church, was originally built in neo-Byzantine style in the 1890s and completed during the first years of the reign of Russia's last Tsar, Nicholas II. Its name stems from the fact that it was built primarily for the use of the Russian Orthodox garrison of nearby Kaunas Fortress, once the largest in the Russian Empire. During the first modern era of Lithuanian independence it became Catholic, temporarily losing this status during the (officially atheist) Soviet period when it was used as an art gallery.

We admired the impressive architecture and the beautiful artworks with a handful of other visitors. It's big, designed as it was to accommodate two thousand worshipers, and as we turned to leave a man in his late middle ages whom I assumed worked there beckoned us to follow him towards a spiral staircase located just inside the front entrance to the church. On the wall was written the enticing word "Crypt," and as we edged forward I could see that the steps descended into complete blackness. I hesitated, but the man urged us forward with a friendly smile as if to say, "Go on, go on, it's okay, friend, for no harm will come to you." We hadn't taken more than a couple of steps down when he pounced, slamming shut a metal-grated door behind us and locking the door with a deft click of a small key that he'd concealed inside his pocket. It seemed we had no choice but to go down; all that was missing from the sense of eeriness was an evil cackle.

It was pitch-black in the basement of the church, and as we gingerly edged ourselves forward we could make out muffled noises in the distance; voices, perhaps, but impossible to tell from our location. It made sense to try and make our way towards them.

"Eurghwhatthehellwasthat!" my dad suddenly exclaimed, without breath or pause. "Something touched me!"

"What was it? Are you alright?"

"Yes, yes, I'm fine. It felt slimy."

This revelation in itself was enough for me to feel positively uncomfortable, so I fumbled in my pockets for what felt like an eternity until my fingers finally grasped my phone. I slid it out carefully so as not to drop it, and switched on the torch setting.

We could see that we were in a narrow passageway, completely covered from top to bottom with rubber gloves of the sort that you might do the washing up in, all sticking out from the walls. This accounted for the slimy contact my father had just experienced. Beyond this the tunnel opened out into a larger room, with random bits of foam and bubble wrap built up in such a way as to form a sort of maze. We headed towards the voices, brushing against a load of beer bottles that had also been stuck against a wall, until eventually we stumbled into a group of Spanish students who had been down there for goodness knows how long. That they screamed with relief when they saw us approach with a light suggests that they had been there for some time.

As we ascended back into the light of day at the head of a now-lengthy procession of people the man who had originally ushered us into the bowels of the church—clearly the warden of this makeshift "sensory maze"—looked thoroughly unimpressed, because it was clear that we had cheated. In fact it transpired that we had been inadvertent guests of the Kaunas Museum for the Blind, which is still open to curious visitors to this day for those who wish to experience a world without sight. I sometimes think that if we hadn't found our way out we'd still be down there now, lost in a web of bin liners and sticky tape like something out of the cult film *Deathline* and its group of feral cannibals living in the depths of the London Underground for generations.

I reached the café first, a pleasant affair right in the bustling heart of Kaunas. I sat myself down at a table near the entrance, keeping my eye on any likely customers who might look like they were there to meet someone. In my haste I suddenly realised that I had no idea what my contact looked like, so it was with some relief when a tall man with glasses and thinning hair approached me and asked if I was "Keet."

Leonidas Donskis was a politician, academic, philosopher, social analyst, author and a nationally respected centre-right commentator; securing his time had helped to make up for the earlier disappointment with Marju Lauristin in Tartu. We shook hands warmly, and I thanked him for joining me.

"Oh, please, it's no bother," he smiled warmly as he sat himself down. The waitress approached and we placed our order. "So how are you finding Kaunas; are you enjoying it?"

I explained that this wasn't my first time in town. He laughed out loud as I told him of the Devil Museum and of our spooky experience under the church. "I must admit that I've never heard of this maze. It sounds like it could be quite the tourist attraction."

Leonidas was originally from Klaipėda—the city on the coast that had once been the Prussian port of Memel—but his academic career had seen him travel widely in Europe and North America and perhaps most exotically during a short stint down the road from Leeds in nearby Bradford. His writings on political theory earned him the title of "Ambassador for Tolerance and Diversity in Lithuania," bestowed by the European Commission in 2004.

After talking through my project in a little more depth he paused for thought for a while and then, with a short "hmm," proceeded with an abbreviated modern history of the Baltics. Lithuania, he explained, differed from Estonia and Latvia, in that the country lacked sizeable minorities—Poles and Jews, once present in large numbers, had all but disappeared due to war and border changes, and Russian speakers had largely sought out industrial opportunities available in Riga and Tallinn. "The Forest Brothers did their bit to scare off Russians as well," Leonidas half-joked.

"And of course," he went on, "it's those large Russian populations in Estonia and Latvia who have created a great deal of nationalist insecurity that just hasn't developed to quite the same degree here in Lithuania. Here there are no 'alien citizens.' But that's not to say we don't share similar problems with the rest of the Baltics. Emigration, for example, is really causing us all concern, and in some ways we have the EU to thank for that. A whole generation is being raised by their grandparents, since their real parents are working abroad.

"And it's problems like emigration and corruption that can sometimes create a lot of nostalgia here, especially for our older people. But also it indicates some naivety, I think; some of us thought that the country would quickly become like Finland or Sweden. I mean, this is definitely a positive time in Lithuania but there is a danger that something has been lost in transition."

Leonidas's anti-Soviet credentials were impeccable; he had been active in the independence movement and made no secret of his distaste of the Soviet system. "But," he pointed out, "it did have some advantages. It was less provincial and parochial, for a start. Academics could co-operate relatively freely across the USSR. And some perspective was lost after independence, because all discourse suddenly had to become nationalist."

It was this last point that I could see made Leonidas angry—very angry. It was obvious that although he saw independence as a profoundly positive development for

Lithuania—a "victory of the Western economic model over the Soviet system"—he was deeply suspicious of how history could be deliberately manipulated in such a way as to present the current political paradigm in a more favourable light.

Nowhere was this more evident, he said, than in Vilnius's Museum of Genocide Victims, which I had visited with my father not long after our initial stay in Kaunas. Leonidas, the son of a Holocaust survivor and who had relatives in Israel, felt that the story of the Holocaust on Lithuanian soil during World War II was being deliberately glossed over in an attempt to cover up an uncomfortable aspect of Lithuania's history. That there was collaboration between the occupying Germans and Lithuanians, he suggested, did not sit comfortably with a narrative of Lithuania and Lithuanians as the sole victims of foreign aggression. "Lithuania wants a heroic past," said Leonidas.

"But all is not lost," he went on. "Young people are beginning to question this narrative now that a whole generation has grown up since independence. And younger people are now less likely to speak Russian there has been a real decrease in the influence of Russian culture, with the knock-on effect of reducing perceptions that Russia is sponsoring some kind of fifth column here, like many people think in Latvia and Estonia."

Leonidas's time was valuable, and so quickly did it pass that in what felt like the blink of an eye we were already shaking hands and wishing each other well. "Good luck with the project," he said as we parted. "Let me know how you get on."

I was enjoying myself in Kaunas. The city is famous across the country for being a city of students, and it has them in abundance; some fifty thousand students attend its various colleges and universities. When it was stripped of its pre-eminent political status after Vilnius had been reacquired during World War II Kaunas successfully reinvented itself as the nation's cultural capital, and was always considered something of a bastion of relative freethinking during the Soviet years. Indeed, the city was the site of a horrific event in May of 1972 when nineteen-year-old student Romas Kalanta set himself on fire in protest against Communist rule. The ensuing rioting over the next few days resulted in hundreds of arrests. A memorial now marks the spot on Laisvės Alėja where the immolation took place.

I found myself staying with a motley bunch of Kaunas's finest not a million miles away from the Garrison Church, on the other side of a leafy park that contained an interesting war memorial from the first era of modern Lithuania's independence. I couldn't help but think that the stone coal-scuttle-helmet-wearing soldier and the numerous crosses of Jagiellons—distinctive crosses with two equal-length horizontal crosspieces—emblazoned all over it made it appear a tad on the authoritarian side. It was ironic, then, that in 2008 Lithuania's parliament passed some of the toughest restrictions anywhere in the former Soviet Union on the display of Nazi and Soviet symbols.

My hosts were Armins, Rasa and Vytis, three extremely laid-back souls who seemed to spend more time smoking weed then actually doing any studying. They all lived together in a cramped but cosy bedsit that, despite being a bit scruffy, still carried the mandatory Lithuanian requirement of leaving one's shoes by the front door. I assumed that I'd be sleeping on a sofa or even on the floor, but I was in luck; a fourth housemate was away for a few days, so I had an entire room to myself. Well, nearly all to myself: Boris the cat had his bed in a corner. He didn't seem to mind sharing with an intruder.

On the night I arrived we decided to take a bike trip, all four of us, to a bar near the Old Town. It felt fantastic to cycle the quiet city streets in the cool midnight air as we took turns taking the lead, weaving in and out of one another's paths with whoops and shrieks. We had one scheduled stop, with an Israeli student who also happened to be the local neighbourhood go-to guy for procuring marijuana, and before long we were at the strangely named BO Bar, which was not all that far from the place Dad and I had stayed several years before.

The three of them were great guys, the very definition of welcoming. Arminas—tall, lanky, spotty and dressed not unlike a hippie—had met me at the bus station, keen to ensure that I wouldn't get lost trying to find my way to their house. Vytis, on the other hand, with his slightly gaunt look and scruffy beard, looked like a likely partner in crime, and as we sat with a beer each he regaled me with his tales of his recent jaunt to somewhere in northern Finland. It was a journey he had completed almost completely by hitchhiking all the way from Kaunas and back again: quite an impressive feat. And Rasa was a little bit quieter but still, every now and then, a flash of a smile or glint of a laugh told me that she was a kind and genuine person too.

The BO Bar was surprisingly busy for a Sunday evening, and before long I had worked out why we had sought out this particular venue. Arminas, it transpired, was something of a pro at foosball, and despite owning a table as a kid and acquiring dubiously strong wrists during my teenage years he proceeded to wipe the floor with me. I hate to think how good he would have been without any "medicinal" stimulants.

BO Bar's other main attraction was a fully set up *Guitar Hero* station, replete with computerised "guitar" to play along in time with the music. On this I fared much better, setting a respectable score in spite of—or perhaps because of—a highly drunken middle-aged lady attempting to dance seductively right in front of me. My very first groupie.

It was a brilliant night. We ate pizza, drank more beers, played more foosball and had an impromptu group photo, courtesy of the drunk woman. By the time we had to cycle back home I'd already realised how lucky I'd been to find such kind, fun and intelligent people. I heard all about student life in Kaunas and their plans for the future: these members of the first generation since independence to grow and blossom into adulthood, their futures filled with an infinite number of possibilities that had been denied their parents and grandparents. They could live, work, study, learn English, and move anywhere they wanted in a Europe that they felt firmly part of—and yet all of them saw their future in Lithuania. "This is a beautiful place and it's our home," mused Arminas wisely in between rounds. I knew exactly what he meant. Perhaps it was the beers, but I knew I'd fallen in love with Lithuania all over again.

When I finally stumbled into my room in the early hours I'd found that the cat had vomited all over my bed.

CHAPTER 9

The Island

* * *

BY THIS POINT I'D BEEN on the road for over a month,
travelling from place to place in an attempt to track down
the remains of the Soviet Union wherever and whenever I
could. I had spoken to a wide range of people from different backgrounds: some born before independence, some
after, and all with their own opinions about the Baltics'
past, present and future. Some felt close to Europe, others
felt an affinity with Russia, and some simply wanted to live
life safe and secure in the knowledge that things would—
or at least should—continue to get better.

My original intention had been to continue to interview
as many people as I could throughout my journey; I had
(with one unfortunate exception) kept to the appointments
I'd arranged prior to setting foot on Baltic soil, and I assumed that the diary would continue to fill as I went along.
But I'd come to the slow realisation as I progressed that
the rate of return for each person I spoke to was becoming
less and less. It wasn't just that the same themes and the

same points of view kept re-emerging; that would surely happen no matter who I met on the trip. It was just that simply speaking to academics and politicians and students was, scientifically speaking, providing too small a sample to accurately gauge whether the views I was hearing really were a genuine reflection of the wider population. Perhaps I simply craved more spontaneity, more variety.

Kaunas was the final prearranged meeting, and I decided there and then that it would be my last. I was extremely grateful to all the people I'd interviewed for taking time out of their days to meet and speak with me, and it was largely because of them that the study's focus had alternated between physical remains of the USSR to societal division and back again. I'd seen a decent swathe of Estonia, Latvia and Lithuania, my route dictated largely by the schedules of those I had spoken to. But now I was a free agent, able to roam wherever I pleased and to follow leads and pick up scents and discover the Soviet Union wherever it could be found. It was, without doubt, all incredibly exciting. But first I needed a break.

I boarded a series of buses all the way to Tallinn, that majestic capital on the shores of the Gulf of Finland. Seeing the glorious spires of the Old Town slide into view once again made my heart soar, this time a sense of familiarity making it almost feel like I was seeing an old friend once again.

I saw Mari a final time, in an open-air rooftop cinema where she was setting up blankets for customers to keep themselves warm during that evening's performance. I wasn't able to stay with her this time; her brother had taken up temporary residence in her apartment as he searched for work in the big city. But it mattered not, for the hug she gave me when we greeted each other was warm and genuine and gave me a little flutter that I prayed was undetectable. So instead we sat awhile and spoke for as long as we could, recounting our various tales since we had last met with laughter and smiles. And then, far too soon, it was time to leave. We hugged again, and as we pulled apart there was a moment—a pause so infinitesimally small and yet feeling like a lifetime—when our eyes met and our movement stopped and we both waited with bated breath. And then it was gone, an opportunity lost and never to return. I couldn't bear to look back as I slowly slunk away.

I was headed for Saaremaa, Estonia's largest island and one of the most ethnically Estonian parts of the country at 97 per cent of the population. In stark contrast to its southern Baltic neighbours, Estonia's coast is littered with hundreds of islands, as if an artist had flicked a giant paintbrush against a canvas of deep ocean blue, each blob and splash a masterpiece in its own right. And fabled Saaremaa, with its grassy meadows bursting with flowers and glorious forests of sweet-smelling pine, is the undisputed queen of these.

It took just a few swift hours to reach the island's capital of Kuressaare, a quick ferry crossing the short distance from the mainland. It was a pleasant journey, the flat islets of the Väike Strait floating by in the breeze as sea and sky merged on the horizon. It was strange to think that this beautiful but also strategically important place had been declared a restricted zone in 1946, off-limits to foreigners and to most mainland Estonians alike. It remained as such until 1989.

I was staying in a hostel a short walk out of town, and after dumping my things I set off to have a look around. Since leaving Tallinn the weather had turned from cloudy skies to murky grey, but despite the odd spit of rain the place was easy on the eye; much of the centre had survived World War II intact, and (the occasional Soviet blemish aside) I found that it had largely retained its historical charm.

But today, for some unknown reason, Kuressaare was like a ghost town. Perhaps it was the threat of rain that kept the streets quiet, but as I wandered around nary a soul was to be seen. As if to confirm my observations the lady in the beautiful town hall tourist office looked genuinely surprised when I casually strolled in, but after quickly composing herself she was happy to furnish me with a map and a few hints and tips on what to see. "It's still out of season," she explained when I queried her about the lack of people around, "so many places will be shut for another week or two."

This included, it transpired, Kuressaare's Episcopal Castle, home of the Saaremaa Regional Museum. I'd heard that the fortress, originally built in the thirteenth century and much altered over the ensuing years, was so well preserved that it looked like something out of a film. It had seen many uses over the centuries, by and large reflecting the shifting fortunes of the island itself: constructed by the Teutonic Order on behalf of the bishops of Ösel-Wieck as part of their efforts to pacify and Christianise the natives, then brief spells of occupation by Denmark and Sweden before being finally absorbed into the Russian Empire. Despite owing much of its present condition to its continuing strategic irrelevance as the Tsars pushed their borders ever westwards, the fortress did see use by both the Nazis and Soviets during their respective ownerships of the island; in Tallinn and Tartu I had seen harrowing photographs of mass graves in the castle's grounds uncovered by Germans forces in 1941 and gleefully seized upon by propagandists. Sadly my view of the fortress was severely obscured by a metal gate, firmly locked with a sturdy-looking padlock.

Not far from the entrance to the castle is a bronze monument of a soldier resting against a rock, with sword drawn and eyes closed in exhaustion. The dates by his feet—1918–1920—reveal that the statue commemorates those islanders who lost their lives in the Estonian War of Independence. Not surprisingly the Soviet authorities weren't too keen on its overtly nationalist tone and were said to have dumped the original into the sea—the figure on display today is a reproduction.

For Saaremaa, despite its deceptively peaceful surroundings, has seen its share of violence over the centuries and particularly during the two World Wars. In 1917 the Imperial German Army captured, as part of Operation Albion, the West Estonian Archipelago (comprising Saaremaa and the neighbouring islands of Hiiumaa and Muhu) in the hope that doing so might open up Saint Petersburg to attack. The islands remained occupied until the end of the war.

World War II was to prove much more costly for Saaremaa. Absorbed into the Soviet Union in 1940 along with the rest of Estonia, the island once again fell under German rule a year later and was the scene of bitter fighting when the Red Army retook it in 1944. The latter was to prove particularly bloody; having given up Hiiumaa and Muhu with barely a whisper the defenders dug in on the Sõrve Peninsula, a long finger of land dangling off Saaremaa's southern coast. Only after several weeks of savage combat, some of it hand-to-hand, did Soviet forces manage to force the evacuation of the German troops. A large Soviet memorial commemorates the Battle of Tehumardi, and even now it's said to be unsafe to walk in undeveloped forest areas on the Sõrve because of the risk of unexploded ordnance leftover from the war.

But I wasn't here to see the memorial. Saaremaa is also famed throughout Estonia as a place of myth and legend; it's here, after all, that the giant Suur Tõll (or "Toell the Great") lived, who had a habit of throwing boulders about the place particularly if his arch-enemy Vanatühi was in the vicinity. After his death it was said that Tõll would have risen again and come to the aid of Saaremaa in case of war, had it not been for a group of naughty children that summoned him back on false pretences. Angered, Tõll returned to his grave and swore never to return—a story which was captured in a wonderfully surreal piece of animation released by the Tallinnfilm studios in 1980. Fortunately I had no need to avail myself of Tõll's services, but there was another mysterious site on Saaremaa that I was extremely curious to see.

A short walk from the hostel brought me to a small garage and bike shop where, courtesy of a kindly woman in her mid-fifties who seemed pleased to have an overseas customer, I picked out a trusty-looking steed to be my transport for the day. One helmet and padlock later—and a shared joke about the distinct lack of mountains in these parts—and I was ready for adventure.

Kaali was little more than a hamlet, and it took me just over an hour to pedal the dozen miles or so from Kuressaare through an idyllic landscape of wide-open meadows punctuated with small stands of birch trees. It was firmly of the blink-and-you'll-miss it variety—there was a village store (closed), a small post office (also closed) and a scattering of houses and farm buildings. And there, incongruously tucked next to a school building, was the crater.

A perfectly round hole in the ground, Kaali's eponymous crater measures over one hundred metres in diameter and is over twenty metres deep. In the centre lies a permanent green lake with barely a ripple disturbing the surface; surrounded by a steep embankment covered with shrubs and trees, it's unusual in that it's fed and maintained almost entirely by rainwater. On a crisp summer morning like today it was a serenely impressive sight, but during times of drought it's been known to be little more than a puddle.

The force that created such a hole was impressive. It's believed that the meteor responsible hit the Earth at around ten miles per second, punching its way into the ground with a strength equivalent to an atomic bomb. Eight other smaller craters pepper the area—formed as the original meteor broke up into pieces in the Earth's atmosphere—but it's the main crater that takes centre stage. For what makes Kaali particularly special is that, at a mere four thousand years old, it's thought to be one of the few such impact craters in the world to be created in the recent past, and the only one to have taken place in a populated area.

At the time of the impact Saaremaa was entering the Nordic Bronze Age. People were starting to form small settlements and communities, and numerous rock-art sites across Scandinavia attest to a period of increasing innovation and expansion. Ongoing contact between different groups led to an ever-increasing exchange of cultural ideas and new technologies; in particular a rich collection of myths and legends began to develop, with epic tales of heroic battles between the gods featuring both in regional mythology and further afield.

It's thought that Kaali features prominently in some of these stories. In nearby Finland, for example, the epic *Kalevala* tells the story of Louhi, a mighty witch-queen capable of changing shape and casting powerful spells.

One day Louhi steals the Sun and fire from mankind, plunging the world into total darkness. Ukko, the god of the sky, orders a new sun to be made from a spark. Ilmatar, the Virgin of the Air, begins to make a new sun but the spark drops from the sky and hits the ground, creating a new lake in its wake.

> *The Sun with a long tail flew with deafening noise over the sky, wood was cut down, trees were set afire and the fortress destroyed. The bright flame of the explosion shook the shores of the Baltic Sea and it was even noticed in faraway countries…*

> *Then it was as quiet as a grave, pitch-dark and only a shimmer from burning forests could be seen. The Sun had fallen down and perished. We couldn't explain it in the other way. But the next day the Sun was in the sky again…*

But rejoice, for all is not lost. Finnish adventurers witness the ball of fire falling somewhere "behind the Neva river"—the direction of Estonia from Finnish Karelia—and after journeying in that direction they are finally able to gather flames from a forest fire.

Another story has it that Saaremaa is the legendary island of Thule. First mentioned by the ancient Greek geographer Pytheas, the theory is that Thule is derived from the Finnic word *tule* ("of fire") and thus ultimately from the folklore of Kalevala. Similarly, the ancient Greek myth of Phaëton tells of the son of Helios who lost control of his chariot of the Sun, scorching the Earth before being struck down by a thunderbolt hurled by Zeus. The meteor strike is also thought to inspire parts of the *Edda*, a prominent collection of medieval Icelandic poems. Notably, Kaali was considered the place where "the sun went to rest."

Whether or not the Kaali meteor was responsible for these legends, archaeology certainly seems to support the claim that the crater enjoyed some sort of sacred status at the time. Thought to have been surrounded by an Iron Age wall almost five hundred metres in length, a large number of domestic animal bones have been found in or around the crater's lake dating from prehistoric times right up until the seventeenth century. It's believed that these sacrifices were offerings to ensure good harvests and that they continued to be made in secret long after the church forbade such paganesque practices. Silver ornaments dating from the first few centuries AD have also been discovered at the site.

Near the crater was the Kaali Visitor Centre, a smart modern building housing a small museum. The receptionist looked genuinely surprised to see me—a phenomenon that I was increasingly getting used to in Saaremaa—and duly jumped into action, racing around the few rooms switching on lights. The displays were mostly dedicated to the geology of the Estonian islands but the museum also featured a more interesting section on the history of the crater, including the moment in 1937 when researchers finally realised that it was created by a meteor and not by volcanic activity as previously thought. It's a display that firmly had its scientific hat on, which was something of a disappointment; little attention was paid to the myths and legends associated with the crater and with the wider island. It seemed a shame.

There wasn't a great deal more to see in Kaali, so I took to the road once more. My guidebook informed me that a short distance to the north were the popular Angla windmills, a series of five venerable windmills standing in a line by the roadside and much loved by passing photographers, so I found the right turning and off I went.

My two wheels propelled me once more through beautiful forests punctuated by wide-open meadows cloaked in flowers of yellow and white. The air carried the beautiful smell of pine, and the sun shone warmly in a blue sky dotted with fluffy white clouds. It was perfect, timeless, gorgeous. And best of all I had this veritable Eden almost entirely to myself, for barely a car conspired to break the solitude.

Still, at the back of my mind I became increasingly conscious of the fact that I'd failed to ensure that I was adequately provisioned; foolishly I'd not brought any food with me from Kuressaare and I'd also not been prepared for Kaali's small café to be closed. I had a little water, but this was also starting to run seriously low.

I slogged on for what felt like miles, slowly beginning to regret my haste and the distance between Saaremaa's rural settlements. Eventually I stumbled across a place with a small village shop; I fell upon its offerings like a man possessed, devouring a multitude of sweet little pastries and a few chocolates, washing it all down with water. Once properly gorged and now feeling slightly refreshed, I looked at the map once more and worked out that I was still a good thirty-minute ride from the windmills, which themselves were around twenty-five miles from the hostel. Taking stock of my situation and adding in the fact that I was feeling firmly on the wrong side of pooped, I decided that I'd chalk this one up to experience. I reluctantly swung the handlebars in the direction of home.

As I plodded my way back to Kuressaare along another hauntingly beautiful road my thoughts turned once again to Kaali. I tried to imagine the "falling of heavenly fire, explosion, clouds of dust and smoke, and the landscape changed beyond recognition (which) must have caused fright and horror and awe among the surviving inhabitants." I realised that it's not beyond the realm of possibility that such a cataclysmic event must have left a lasting impression upon the people of the island, and that stories of the sun falling from the sky spread to other cultures as trade and warfare across the region grew. Perhaps the most tangible legacy of the Kaali meteor is perhaps not found in the crater that bears its name but in the numerous stories and legends that find their origins in this most peaceful of places.

My sojourn in Saaremaa had been a lovely one, for I had been privileged enough to spend a few precious days in an enchanting landscape that often felt like time had stood still for centuries. Its sylvan landscape was wonderfully simple and yet pleasing beyond words; I could have spent days, weeks even, exploring its winding lanes and enchanting forests. Little wonder, then, that it holds a special place in Estonian national consciousness as a pure and peaceful idyll free from the pressures of modern urban life. Perhaps the fact that it is an island helps to cement its status as a place apart.

Yet interestingly this entire stretch of coast was once home to a much more diverse array of peoples than its current position as a bastion of Estonian culture might suggest. For centuries a small population of Swedes lived in and amongst the many islands of western Estonia. These Rannarootslased—or "Coastal Swedes," as they were termed by their Estonian neighbours—began arriving in small numbers during the thirteenth century, only for the trickle to become a flood when Sweden captured the island (then known as Ösel) from Denmark in 1645. Swedish rule in Ösel and in the greater part of the Baltics would last for another sixty-five years before eventual capitulation to

Peter the Great's forces during the closing stages of the Great Northern War.

But even after its incorporation into the Russian Empire small numbers of Estonian Swedes continued to eke out a living, despite the loss of their previously privileged position and the threat of the occasional expulsion (all the ethnic Swedes on Hiiumaa were forcibly relocated to Ukraine by Catherine the Great.) Never numbering more than ten thousand souls out of a national population of a million, the vast majority fled to Sweden during the Second World War, never to return. Today just a handful of people in Estonia can claim Rannarootslased descent, but there has been a noticeable upswing in interest in Swedish heritage and culture since independence. The flag of the Swedish Estonians—three horizontal stripes of blue, black and yellow—is an intentional fusion of the flags of their dual homelands.

More significant than the Swedes, and certainly far more influential, were the aristocratic Baltic Germans. For centuries the ethnic German populace, despite never making up more than a tenth of the total population, almost exclusively comprised *the* social, commercial, political and cultural elite of the region. First arriving with the Livonian crusaders of the thirteenth century, Baltic Germans came to play a preeminent role in the military and civilian life of the Russian Empire, particularly in Saint Petersburg; individuals such as Field Marshall Michael Barclay de Tolly, explorer Ferdinand von Wrangel and Peter Carl Fabergé (of egg fame) cemented an ethnic German impact out of all proportion to their numbers. Their domination over so much of Baltic life helped ensure that German was considered the language of the ruling classes right up until World War I.

Whilst the first round of Baltic independence witnessed an abrupt end to their enviable position, many Baltic Germans chose to stay, opting to contribute in the process to the cultural and political life of the new Estonian, Latvian and Lithuanian republics. Yet the days of the Germans were numbered. In late 1939, following the signing of the Molotov-Ribbentrop Pact, almost all the Baltic Germans were resettled by the Hitler regime to occupied Poland under the *Heim ins Reich* programme as part of the twin Nazi efforts to colonise their newly acquired territories and to bring all ethnic Germans into a single German Reich. At the end of the war, most of them were expelled—as were most Germans who were left stranded east of the Oder-Neisse Line—into what was left of the rump German state.

Still, I knew my time in Saaremaa, and in Estonia for that matter, was coming to a close. I boarded the bus back to Tallinn and barely gave the place a second glance as I hopped on a transfer to Riga. A night at Kristīne's later and then I was back in Lithuania, refreshed and invigorated and determined to do justice to this largest and most southerly of the Baltics.

CHAPTER 10

Stone Soldiers

✳ ✳ ✳

PERCHED HIGH ATOP A HILL a couple of miles and a
short ride in a rickety trolley bus from the centre of
town is Vilnius's Television Tower, the tallest structure
in Lithuania, still in use as the home of the Lithuanian
Radio and Television Centre. Its long slender structure
can be seen all over the city, and on a clear day it's possible from the summit to see as far as Elektrėnai, the
Soviet-era town purpose-built for the workers of its power station some thirty miles away.

Sadly I wasn't going to see Elektrėnai or anything else
for that matter, for fate had decided that of all the days I
would choose to go up the tower, today would be the wet-
test of the trip. Dark soggy clouds hung heavy in the sky,
soaking everyone and everything not fortunate enough to
find shelter and completely obscuring the revolving observation deck (replete with obligatory café) in the process. Such conditions meant that access to the public was
strictly and disappointingly restricted to the ground floor.

But it's not its height or views from the top that marks the tower as especially significant. It was here, in January of 1991, that fourteen unarmed civilians lost their lives in an attempt to prevent the Soviet military from entering the mast. Reports of the killings flashed around the world, fatally tarnishing the Gorbachev regime and boosting the Baltics' fledgling independence movements in the process.

Throughout the late 1980s independence activists across the Baltics were becoming increasingly emboldened as the Soviet system slowly began to crumble, a situation inadvertently exacerbated by the local Communist Parties' collective reluctance to embrace perestroika and glasnost. In 1989 these activists staged possibly their most audacious demonstration to date: a human chain, two million strong, stretching all the way from Tallinn to Riga and Vilnius. The "Baltic Way" aimed both to bring the situation in the Baltics to the attention of the world and to reaffirm Baltic solidarity: ambitions that the demonstration spectacularly achieved. The twenty-third of August—the date of the Chain and the anniversary of the Molotov-Ribbentrop Pact—has since become an official remembrance day in the Baltic states and across the European Union.

The end of the 1980s and the dawn of a new decade saw no let-up; a huge pro-independence rally in the centre of Vilnius greeted Gorbachev during a brief visit in January of 1990, and shortly afterward the first free elections in the Soviet Union returned majorities for secessionist groups in all three of the Baltic states. In Lithuania the victorious Sąjūdis Party led from the front, unilaterally declaring independence from Moscow on the eleventh of March. Estonia and Latvia followed shortly after.

The first few months of this unofficial "independence" were extremely difficult for Lithuania. Inflation reached 100 per cent, and a Soviet economic blockade contributed to shortages of both energy supplies and basic goods. Many of the minority Russians and Poles in the country, made uneasy by the unilateral nature of the declaration and what they perceived to be ethnic discrimination in the workplace and elsewhere, also expressed discontent

Tensions rose sharply in the first few days of 1991. Protests by workers over continuing price hikes soon turned into broader protests in support of the pro-Moscow Yedinstvo movement. A rally in front of the Supreme Council of Lithuania turned violent as protesters attempted to storm the parliament buildings; they were repelled by water cannons, prompting Chairman of Parliament (and de facto head of state) Vytautas Landsbergis to publicly call for supporters of independence to protect public buildings. Alarmed by the spiralling disorder Gorbachev—who still refused to recognise Baltic independence—sent in troops in an attempt to restore the (Soviet) rule of law. Events moved quickly; Soviet forces began securing sites of strategic interest all over the country and the local Communist Party quickly announced that it was once again the only legitimate government in Lithuania.

In the early hours of the thirteenth of January word spread that tanks were heading for the Television Tower, which by now was full of independence supporters who had heeded Landsbergis's call. When the tanks arrived an initial salvo of blanks failed to disperse the crowds, which prompted soldiers to fire live rounds, killing almost a dozen demonstrators. Two would be crushed by the tanks.

It was all completely pointless. Once in control of the tower, the Soviets closed down the TV service—only for it to promptly switch to broadcasting from studios in Kaunas. Fearful of causing further casualties the military backed down, but the damage was already done; international reaction overwhelmingly condemned the disproportionate use of force, signalling the beginning of the end. In a referendum on independence held a month later in which 85 per cent of the population voted, 90 per cent voted in favour of independence.

At the foot of the tower stands a small group of wooden crosses commemorating the dead of January 13, along with a concrete slab listing the names of those who lost their lives. The drip-drip of the rain made the memorial all the more sombre, a *rūpintojėlis* metaphorically shedding a tear for the fourteen. Only a bright yellow flower at the monument's base offered any respite from the drabness.

The ground floor of the Tower contains a small museum dedicated to the events of that night, tucked away at the back behind the main reception. Fortunately it was open, and I spent a while attempting to take in the drama played out in the photos that made up the bulk of the exhibits. The images of the funerals that took place in the centre of Vilnius and of the thousands who attended did something to convey the raw emotion of that time, but it was the black-and-white photos of the victims that stood out the most—each one to be remembered for all eternity as heroes and martyrs of the independence movement. Today many of the streets around the Tower carry their names.

I also noticed a small plaque that had been fixed, almost as an afterthought, to one of the panels informing visitors that the exhibits were mostly the property of the Museum of Genocide Victims. The notice directed those interested in the Holocaust and the Nazi occupation of Lithuania to the Vilna Gaon Jewish State Museum. Perhaps Leonidas's wishes for the history of the extermination of Lithuania's Jews to be given due prominence was starting to gain traction with the powers that be.

Despite the rain Vilnius was as glorious as I remembered. It felt simply marvellous to be wandering through its narrow cobbled streets once again, and—just as in my first visit a few years before—my heart skipped a beat as I emerged from the warrens of the Old Town into Cathedral Square, with its beautiful free-standing belfry and imposing statue of Gediminas, the legendary founder of Lithuania. It was here, at the very centre of Lithuanian Christianity, that the crowds would gather night after night in the run-up to independence, and where the emotionally charged funerals of those killed at the Television Tower were held.

The historic heart of Vilnius lies to the south of the River Neris, which meanders gracefully through the city and offers the perfect frame to what is probably the finest collection of baroque architecture in northern Europe. Some of the best views of town can be had from the Gediminas Tower, a red-brick edifice that sits in a commanding position on a hill overlooking the city and is one of the city's best-known landmarks. The panorama offers the perfect reward for the heart-pounding walk up to the tower's ramparts.

In fact Vilnius is surprisingly hilly—something of a novelty in the low-lying Baltics, and not far from the Tower and the bustling city centre is the lovely Kalnų Park, a haven of peaceful tranquillity that I was irresistibly drawn to. A paved path took me through pleasing hillocks covered with pine trees, and since it was the weekend I shared it with a teeming multitude of families, lovers, joggers, old and young: all making the most of this enchanting place right on their doorstep. Eventually I emerged at the Hill of Three Crosses, most prominent of Kalnų's "peaks." Tradition has it that Jogaila—the last pagan ruler of Lithuania and the man responsible for the country's conversion to Catholicism, as well as for laying the foundations of the Polish-Lithuanian Union—erected three giant crosses here in memory of several Franciscan monks executed at this spot by his grandfather. Whether he did so or not, what is certain is that a trio of crosses did exist here until their removal by the Tsarist authorities as a response to the January Uprising against Russian rule in 1863. A bizarre game of cat-and-mouse then ensued; when the Russians withdrew during the First World War the city raised new crosses in celebration, only for the Soviets to subsequently blow them up in 1950. The latest incarnation—three gleaming white crosses that stand in a magnificent spot over the eastern part of the city—were erected shortly before the most recent round of Lithuanian independence. The view from their base takes in the entire Old Town and farther afield, of red-tiled rooftops and green trees punctuated by soaring church spires. Only on the distant horizon could I spy anything resembling a tower block. It occurred to me that whilst the Soviets had managed to earn themselves the unenviable reputation of specialising in bland and conformist architecture they did at least have the sense to leave the centres of the Baltic capitals largely unaltered.

Indeed, it would be easy to navigate around the centre of the city without really being aware of walking on what was once Soviet soil, as integral a part of the Union as Moscow or Saint Petersburg. Little now indicates that this was ever the case since any hint of Soviet history is hidden away, revealing itself only in subtle ways to those who seek to uncover it. I had seen the hammer-and-sickle in Tallinn and Kaunas, manhole covers bearing Cyrillic script in Tartu and heroic statuary in Riga—but here in

Vilnius Communist symbols were made conspicuous by their absence.

What was until recently a noticeable exception is the Green Bridge. A structure has existed at roughly this location on the Neris since the sixteenth century but—reflecting the tumultuous history of this land—the crossing has been destroyed and rebuilt numerous times throughout its history. The present span was completed in 1952 after being blown up by retreating Wehrmacht troops during the war; it was renamed for a Soviet general before reverting to its historical name once again upon independence. The bridge is, as you might expect, painted in a pleasing shade of forest green.

What made the bridge stand out, however, were the four sculptures standing at each of its corners. Erected in 1952, they were prominent examples of Soviet realism featuring soldiers, workers, farmers and students—all classes idealised and extolled by the Communist authorities. From the moment of independence debate raged over their future, with those who viewed the statues as historically significant pitted against self-styled patriots who wished to see no visible reminders of the Soviet period. The latter eventually won out, and in July 2015 the statues were taken down for good. The city authorities denied that their removal was politically motivated, claiming that health and safety concerns demanded that the ageing monuments could remain no longer. The mask slipped, however, when the mayor of Vilnius declared that "The statues represent a lie. Their heroic portrayal of the Soviet people—that is all a lie…The statues are a mockery of the real people who had to live during the Soviet period."

I remember seeing them *in situ* the first time I visited Lithuania. I have to admit that in their own way I thought them rather marvellous, capturing perfectly the ideological mood of the times. Given the increasing difficulty in viewing such statues in their original setting it made me sad to find them gone—but perhaps that demonstrates an insensitivity to local feelings. Whatever the truth of the matter it was interesting to note that they were all crafted locally, each by a different Lithuanian designer, and not by incomers from other parts of the Soviet Union. I wondered: Did the contemporary political climate make them any less Lithuanian?

But the Soviet history of Vilnius can be uncovered in other ways. Running in an arrow-straight line from Cathedral Square to the squat Soviet-era Parliament Building (the Seimas) and the Neris is Gedimino prospektas, the city's main thoroughfare in Tsarist times and today the place where trendy young things come to shop and do business. Its successive name changes over the years— Saint George, Mickiewicz, Stalin and Lenin at different points all referenced—reflect the various regimes that have held sway here. Indeed Lenin once held permanent audience in Lukiškės Square, on the northern side of the street, until his statue was unceremoniously removed and dumped in August 1991. The square was also the site of the public hanging of anti-Russian rebels in the nineteenth century.

Opposite the square is the squat, brooding neoclassical edifice that is the former headquarters of both the KGB and the Gestapo and which is now the home of the Museum of Genocide Victims. As I walked along its solid grey walls I counted dozens and dozens of names etched into its surface in testament to those who had suffered and died within.

Inside was much as I remembered from the first time I visited. Various rooms on the ground floor told the story of the Soviet period—from the initial incorporation of Lithuania into the USSR in 1940 and the period immediately after the expulsion of the Nazis right through to the fall of Communist power—in a similar vein to those of its sister institutions in Estonia and Latvia. I heard about partisans and Forest Brothers, of deportations and arbitrary arrests—a systematic programme of repression with roots in the Russification agenda of the Tsars. The section on the "People's Defenders" was particularly interesting; these were Lithuanian pro-Soviet partisans who, according to the museum, were hated by the indigenous population and who were guilty of numerous atrocities, in complete contrast (of course) to the heroic Forest Brothers despite the latter's propensity to inflict "some violence against the civilian population...as in any war." It was hard to escape the nagging doubt that this was not a completely impartial description of history.

Upstairs was a recreation of the self-congratulatory KGB museum that had once been open only to members of the organisation; I looked closely at the photographs that adorned the walls and display cabinets, noting how many of them had Lithuanian names. I was curious to know how these local recruits would have fared in a post-independence Lithuania: would they be forever tarred as sell-outs or collaborators, traitors to their nation? Would they have had to flee, either to Russia or elsewhere? Or were so many involved in administering the regime that their rehabilitation was necessitated by the pragmatic needs of the newly independent authorities?

The real shock of the museum, however, is contained in its dingy basement, which has been preserved largely as it was when the KGB withdrew in 1991. Here the visitor may find cells where people were imprisoned and tortured for days on end or sometimes made to stand on a small wooden disc surrounded by freezing-cold water for hours at a time. Particularly chilling was the padded cell; the thought of prisoners screaming but unheard from the outside positively made my skin crawl.

Another flight of stairs down brought me into a cold and gloomy space where an intensely dispiriting scene from the 2007 film *Katyn* was playing on a loop. It featured soldiers of the Polish Republic, bound at the wrists, being frog-marched into a dingy-looking building by sneering Soviets and shot once in the back of the head in a room that looked much like the one I was standing in.

Their bodies were then hauled along a trough through an opening in the wall to a waiting cart stacked high with corpses.

Katyn is the name for a notorious series of massacres that took place during the Second World War. Soviet forces, fearful of a strong Polish state, set out to systematically erase most of the army's officer class and intelligentsia captured during the initial occupation of eastern Poland in 1939 and 1940. The total number of victims is estimated at around twenty-two thousand, mostly executed in the Katyn Forest near Smolensk but also in Kalinin and Kharkiv Prisons and elsewhere.

When their remains were subsequently disinterred by occupying Nazi troops the Germans instantly saw their propaganda potential, eagerly exploiting this indisputable evidence of Bolshevik barbarity for their own nefarious purposes by inviting a Red Cross committee to inspect the site. Grainy newsreels showed mass graves stacked high with bodies and skulls punctured with bullet-shaped holes, as well as clothing and other items—all testimony to the terrible crimes that had taken place. The Soviet government immediately denied the charges and instead blamed the Nazis for the killings.

In 1943, as the Red Army pushed back the front line, they once again came into ownership of Katyn—and immediately set about faking evidence to suggest that the killings had taken place during the German occupation and not in 1940, when it had still been controlled by the

Soviets. Investigation teams sent by Moscow conveniently concluded that it was a German atrocity; only in 1990 did the Soviet authorities finally accept responsibility for what had happened at Katyn.

Curiously, this would not be the last time that senior Polish officials would be killed in the area. In 2010 an aeroplane carrying Polish President Lech Kaczyński with his wife, other politicians, and several high-ranking army officers crashed in thick fog on its way to Smolensk for a ceremony to mark the seventieth anniversary of the massacre. All ninety-six on-board were killed in an event that stunned the Polish nation.

While Katyn was largely a Polish tragedy the parallels being drawn by playing the film—itself criticised in some quarters for its one-dimensional portrayal of evil Soviet troops—in the museum's basement were obvious. Here, in the depths of the KGB headquarters where opponents of the regime were executed, the Soviet Union brutally repressed those who dared to stand in its way.

Vilnius has other links to the Soviet security services. In the eastern district of Užupis a young Felix Dzerzhinsky lived as a high-school student before moving on to become a Bolshevist agitator in Kaunas. "Iron" Felix was a Polish aristocrat born in what is now modern-day Belarus who gained notoriety as the founder of the Cheka, the forerunner of the KGB; as its first director he oversaw its central role in the Red Terror, the campaign of mass killings, torture, and systematic oppression that was carried out immediately after the Russian Revolution. I remembered seeing a statue of him in Minsk, a surprise even there considering Dzerzhinsky's overt role in the repression of the masses and his corresponding veneration by Stalin; his imposing statue in Moscow's Lubyanka Square, after all, was permanently removed to much cheering in 1991. Perhaps less surprising is that Užupis is equally silent when it comes to commemorating its former resident.

Despite these connotations Užupis is an interesting part of the city, crystallising the quirky streak that cuts its merry way through the Baltics. Not far from the Three Crosses and sharing the hilly aspect of its neighbour, its name literally means "across the river." The area is separated from the Old Town by the Vilnia, the much more modest of Vilnius's two rivers and quite probably the source of the city's name. Užupis is also the spiritual heart of the country's bohemian movement: in 2000 the district declared itself independent as the Republic of Užupis, replete with its own flag, currency, president, cabinet of ministers and constitution. Meant as a wry commentary on commercialism and globalisation, artistic endeavour is nevertheless one of the key outputs of the republic as is the strengthening of community links and the stimulating of local culture. Not far from a statue of Mickiewicz whimsical border signs at the entrance to Užupis feature a Mona Lisa and a smiley-face logo—and all without a bribe-happy border guard in sight. I felt that there was something to be said for "countries" like these.

I made my way ever farther eastwards to where the sub-urbs of Vilnius began to fracture and melt into a gorgeous slice of woodland—the Pavilnių regioninis parkas—which serves as a haven of peaceful tranquillity almost as large as the city itself. I was seeking out Antakalnis Cemetery, and with a bit of effort I found the entrance to it tucked behind some nondescript housing some way off the main road. It sat in complete contrast to the relatively mundane urban space I had just walked through; here beams of sunshine pierced through tall trees and all the noise and stress of the town seemed to melt into timeless nothingness. It was and is simply a beautiful place to walk, to reflect and to remember.

For Antakalnis means different things to different people. Twelve of the fourteen killed at the Television Tower are buried here, as are the border guards killed in what is known as the Medininkai incident, when members of the Lithuanian State Border Guards were attacked by a Soviet regime that regarded such an institution as illegal. They are collectively commemorated by the Memorial of the January Events' Victims, a moving monument based in a clearing near the centre of the cemetery. The presence of these graves—of martyrs in the story of Lithuania's fight for independence from Soviet rule—firmly ce-ments Antakalnis's position as a place of pilgrimage for Lithuanian nationalists and their supporters.

And yet Antakalnis is also home to many nationalities and many ideologies that have fought and died over this contested patch of land. I saw what seemed like hundreds of grey crosses, as high as my knee, carpeting a small meadow like a silent crop of stone poppies. The red-and-white bands carefully wrapped around each one revealed the identity of their occupants: Poles, killed in the tug-of-war-fighting after the end of the First World War that would ultimately result in the city's occupation by Polish troops and eventual annexation by Poland in 1922. Another memorial commemorates German and Russian troops also killed in what was known at the time as the Great War.

But perhaps most surprising is that Antakalnis is home to a grandiose memorial to the Red Army. In the glorious sunshine it was an impressive sight to behold: at the head of a long stepped platform cut into a natural dip between hillocks and flanked by huge stone dates reading "1941" and "1945" stood six giant soldiers, all with the firm square jaws beloved by socialist realism. They were carved from solid rock and stared directly ahead, fixed and unwavering, as if they were silently emerging from the cloak of pine trees behind them. Nearby stone tablets recorded the names of the dead—in both Lithuanian and Russian—all with dates ending in the first half of the 1940s, lost in some of the bloodiest fighting in the Great Patriotic War. What struck me most, just as with the rest of the cemetery, was how well maintained the monument was; not a blade of grass was out of place and every headstone looked clean and fresh. Even the landscaped trees were perfectly manicured. Despite the differences in culture, nationality, language, religion and ideology, here was a place where all were equal and all could find eternal rest.

As I sat awhile to take in the gently warm surroundings I watched as two young children, barely older than four or five, clambered and played in and out of the stones in blissful ignorance of the sacrifice that had gone before. It may have been a wonderfully clichéd scene but it still made me sorely hope that they would never have to endure the suffering of those previous generations interred at Antakalnis.

Many visitors to Vilnius head out to Trakai, a pretty town some twenty miles or so from the capital that is chiefly famous for its fairy-tale lakeside castle and as the historic centre of Lithuania's Karaim community—Turkic-speaking Jews originating from Crimea who were invited to the region in the late fourteenth century. I decided to skip the crowds, however, and instead jumped on a train to the unremarkable suburb of Paneriai. I say "unremarkable," because but for one event this wooded area would no doubt continue to slumber on in peaceful anonymity. For three long, horrific years from 1941 to 1944 some one hundred thousand people—chiefly Jews but also Russians, Poles, political prisoners and various other "undesirables"—were killed and buried at Paneriai by the occupying Nazis in what is known as the Ponary Massacre.

The entrance to the killing grounds are found down a road that runs directly from the railway station through the forest; on an overcast day like today the water in the air couldn't fail to bring out the vivid freshness of the pines. After a mile or so of trudging I came to a large car park which was empty and deserted, with room enough for coaches and smaller vehicles yet completely devoid of visitors. All was quiet—eerily so. The place felt like it had simply been abandoned and forgotten long ago.

It's perhaps this innocuous introduction to Paneriai that seems so jarring and so unreal: that a short walk through such peaceful surroundings can transport you to a place that was the site of unmitigated horror. There are around half a dozen pits, connected to one another by a series of pathways like some gigantic spider's web. They had originally been dug by the Soviets to use as oil dumps, but, unlike at Katyn, it was the Nazis—along with the *Ypatingasis būrys* units made up of locally recruited Lithuanian collaborators—who saw their potential as mass graves with convenient transport links to the rest of Germany's aforementioned Reichskommissariat Ostland. Each separate pit is marked by a stone monument inscribed in both Latvian and Russian recording the unspeakable things that happened there; I subsequently learned that one told of innumerable burned corpses dumped by Nazis.

There was a scattering of other monuments as well; most were Soviet but others dated from later periods. I spotted one bedecked with Polish colours—it was clearly much newer, dating from the turn of the millennium. The tiny on-site museum was closed, but I felt myself pause awhile as I watched a small bird fly to and from a small hole in the rafters, hungry squawks emanating from within, which gave me no doubt as to the cause of its frenetic activity.

At the side of the car park stood a couple of stark stone monoliths. One simply read "Paneriai" in heavy solid letters, whilst the other appeared to be made up of what was once a single block split in two by an additional stone inscription, placed there as if merely an afterthought. In many ways this is exactly what happened; the older horizontal block records the murder of specifically "Soviet" citizens at the site—citizens involuntarily afforded that status by a regime that itself had taken control of Lithuanian lands under exceedingly dubious circumstances.

And yet it was the newer inscription that was perhaps the more revealing, for it was written in Hebrew and bore the Star of David in recognition of the vast majority of the victims who were Jewish. This great boulder was only added in 1990, in belated recognition of the fact that the suffering of the Jews under the Nazi regime was often deliberately downplayed long after the event.

Paneriai is by no means unique in this regard. At Babi Yar, the ravine in the Ukrainian capital of Kiev where thirty-four thousand Jews were shot by the occupying Germans over a two-day period in 1941, no specifically Jewish commemoration efforts were permitted until the country became an independent nation in 1991. And in the small Russian town of Nevel, not far from the border with Belarus, a six-pointed Star of David on a memorial to the murdered Jewish inhabitants that once called this place home was deliberately defaced so that it had only five points—in imitation of the star of the Soviet Union.

In many ways this policy might seem odd. It should be remembered that the mass murder of Europe's Jews and other "undesirables" by the Nazis marked a huge demographic shift in the lands stretching from the Baltics all the way down to the Black Sea, a vast area once known as the "Pale of Settlement." This was the only region of imperial Russia where Jews were allowed to permanently settle and beyond which they were generally prohibited. This was an ethnically diverse area, with populations of Jews, Orthodox Christians and Catholics all living more or less side-by-side. Originally this was in *shtetls*—towns with high proportions of Jews of the sort portrayed in *Fiddler on the Roof*—but as industrialisation set in increasing numbers migrated to the large cities of the empire's north-western reaches and in particular Poland and Lithuania.

Life in the Pale was not easy, however, and the authorities often turned a blind eye to vicious anti-Semitism in the form of violent pogroms. It's more than possible that the legacy of the pogroms helped to fuel the connivance of those locals who were all too eager to assist the Einsatzgruppen in their efforts to wipe the Jews from the face of the earth.

Yet the Soviets—who, as Katyn demonstrated, were happy to seize upon any potential propaganda to attack and undermine their foe—did little to highlight Jewish suffering under the Nazi jackboot. As atheists it would have been anathema for the Communists to commemorate the suffering of any individual religious group, even though it was the Jews who were specifically targeted and executed on what Moscow considered to be sovereign Soviet soil. And the statistics really do make for grim reading: in Vilnius, only 10 per cent of the city's seventy thousand Jews survived the war; in Kaunas, the pre-war Jewish population of thirty-five thousand was reduced to a mere handful and only around a thousand remain in the city today.

But I also wondered if this Soviet legacy—the notion that the Jews of the Second World War suffered no more and no less than any other citizens of the USSR—was a reaction to claims by Nazi Germany and others that Bolshevism was a world-wide Jewish conspiracy, part of some great master plan to take over the world. Or perhaps there was a fear that acknowledging Jewish suffering under German rule would have meant some navel-gazing of their own: that at least some recognition of the damage their own pogroms caused would also be required. Perhaps it was a fear that others—whether it be Poles or Jews—may retain a stake in the newly acquired lands of the Kresy. Whatever the cause, at Paneriai the newly independent Lithuanian authorities were keen to rectify a historical wrong: self-serving, perhaps, given the scale of local collaboration that took place, but important nonetheless.

Yet others would argue that it was the Soviet Union that did more to save European Jewry from obliteration than any other nation. Marc Chagall, the Belarus-born Jewish painter who fled to the United States from France during the war, was unwavering in his defence of the Motherland's record:

> *The Jews will always be grateful to* [the Soviet Union]. *What other great country has saved a million and a half Jews from Hitler's hands, and shared its last piece of bread? What country abolished antisemitism? What other country devoted at least a piece of land as an autonomous region for Jews who want to live there? All this, and more, weighs heavily on the scales of history.*

Stalin's World

* * *

I WAS UP EARLY, EAGER to catch the bus that would spirit me away to Druskininkai, the southernmost town in Lithuania and hence of all the Baltic states. By now the weather had taken a turn for the better, and so it was that I sat with a smile as we made our way along quiet tree-lined roads, punctuated only by cutesy villages like something straight out of a fairy-tale.

The name of the settlement comes from the Lithuanian word *druska*, meaning "salt," a reference to the mineral-rich spring waters which cemented the reputation of the otherwise innocuous Druskininkai as one of the Soviet Union's foremost spa towns. At one time over one hundred thousand people would flock here every year in the hope that the curative waters would treat ailments ranging from heart disease to asthma, bronchitis and a myriad of other morbidities. Since the demise of the USSR the numbers have decreased substantially but many still come to avail themselves of the many beauty and wellness treatments—although in this age of capitalist consumerism such services are no longer free.

Walking around it was easy to see why people from all over Lithuania and beyond come here to relax and to escape the stresses and strains of modern life. It wasn't that the buildings were particularly pretty; on the contrary, apart from the attractive blue Orthodox church in the centre of town and a smattering of other Tsarist-era offerings everything looked fairly modern. But what marked Druskininkai as a little bit special was the way in which it just seemed to merge with the surrounding forest, as if the trees had simply parted to allow the houses and the roads to be built between them. Trees were simply everywhere, and the very air felt like it had been touched with the fragrance of pine and birch. Throw in a couple of lakes and you had the perfect spot in which to while away a few days.

I hadn't come to Druskininkai to relax, though, as tempting as that would have been. After spending a pleasant time simply enjoying the calmness of it all I decided to hop on another bus to go a couple of miles back up the road on which I had travelled just a short while before to the small village of Grūtas.

There isn't a great deal to see in Grūtas itself: a few quiet streets, some well-kept houses and another picture-postcard lake on the other side of the main road. But tucked away behind the village is another kind of attraction altogether, one that proved immensely controversial when it first opened its doors: Grūtas Park, more popularly known as Stalin World.

As communist regimes fell like dominos all over Europe the newly emancipated people faced a huge number of problems, not least of which was what to do with all the Soviet statues that could be found in every town and city across the Baltics. The obvious answer for the exuberant crowds was to simply tear down the Lenins and triumphant workers and hammer-and-sickle motifs in an orgy of iconoclasm, and in many cases this is exactly what happened. The world watched on in awe at this potent symbol of regime change—for with the downing of the statues came the real recognition that Soviet authority had simply ceased to exist in any legitimate or practical form. Many of these monuments were subsequently lost or destroyed, or ended up sitting in storage gathering dust. Some, however, were snapped up by collectors keen to preserve a moment of history—either for sentimental reasons or simply for profit.

The latter motive largely explains why the small village of Grūtas is now home to what is probably the biggest collection of Soviet statues on public display in the Baltics. In the mid-1990s a prominent local businessman saw in the unwanted figures an opportunity to open a park that would both tell the story of Lithuania under Communism and transform the statues into a tourist attraction at the same time. But the park's opening caused such a storm of controversy that purported plans to include a train ride in cattle trucks similar to those once used to deport Lithuanians to Siberia had to be abandoned for fear of trivialising the national experience under Communist rule. Whether contrived or otherwise, the furore around the so-called Soviet Disneyland and the apparent insensitivity to national suffering provided a massive publicity boost, and today Grūtas Park is the biggest tourist attraction in southern Lithuania—a fact surely not unappreciated by the hoteliers and restaurateurs of nearby Druskininkai.

Despite this apparent popularity, however, it all seemed fairly quiet when I visited, with only the occasional visitor, a zebra and couple of donkeys from the on-site zoo disturbing the tranquillity—a fact of which I was not in the least resentful as it only served to underline how beautiful its setting is. For the location of the park, it has to be said, is really rather nice, standing as it does right next to another of the multitude of small lakes that dot the region. With a spring in my step I paid my fee to the lady in the booth by the entrance—smiles were clearly not included in the ticket price—and pushed my way through a metal gate emblazoned with the arms of the Lithuanian Soviet Socialist Republic. I knew I was going to like it here.

I once visited a similar site near Budapest called "Memento Park" that, while considerably busier, was really just a collection of statues and little else by way of context or explanation. Grūtas Park, however, was much more immersive; a path takes visitors on a roughly circular forested route dotted with statues and re-creations of watchtowers and lines of barbed-wire fences, all with explanatory panels offering a crash course in Soviet history. The usual suspects were there: Lenin, Stalin, Dzerzhinsky, Red Army soldiers, Soviet partisans and other home-grown notables from the interwar Lithuanian revolutionary movement, as well as a scattering of vehicles—including *those* cattle cars—and other associated memorabilia. Of particular interest was the giant Lenin with the missing thumb and what looked like two large horizontal scars just below his knees—the place where, in August 1991, he was cut down and unceremoniously hauled away by a crane from where he had once stood proud in the centre of Vilnius.

But the figure that struck me the most was at first glance much less notable than its neighbours. It was a stylised bust of Stefanija Greiciute, a local teenager who, I learned, had been heavily involved with various Communist youth organisations. Her features, embossed in a somewhat abstract manner in a solid block of red stone and staring out with unnervingly blank pupil-less eyes, commemorated the fact that she had been killed by the Lithuanian Forest Brothers as a Soviet collaborator—the very same partisans who were now celebrated as heroes in contemporary discourse all across the Baltics. This got me thinking; that the dominant political ethos of the day either renders such action an act of defiance or one of terrorism. For the regime of the time Stefanija's murder for her ideological convictions would have ensured her eternal martyrdom, whereas today's nationalism casts doubt on whether Stefanija was a victim at all, killed as she was in the sacred struggle against Communist rule. Whatever the merits of either argument, it made me profoundly sad that the murder of someone so young could ever be considered a legitimate act. That earlier description of the Brothers' activities rang loud in my ears: "Some violence against the civilian population occurred, as in any war."

Grūtas Park was not finished with me yet. In the centre of the complex stood a couple of wooden huts containing old photos, films, newspaper clippings and propaganda posters exhorting the masses to work harder for the greater good of the state—some were even aimed at schoolchildren, instructing them to love the Party as much as they did their own parents. And during the busy summer months actors at the park dressed in period uniform would be on hand to explain what life was like in Soviet times, in between marching around the site to rousing music and slogans played over the loudspeaker system. Somewhat disappointingly they failed to appear during my visit.

After a good couple of hours I reluctantly decided to bid farewell to what I thought was a tasteful and purposeful site. The "Stalin World" tag seemed unfair to me, for this was no mere theme park: I found no celebration or trivialisation of Soviet rule at Grūtas. Instead it was preserving and presenting an important period of Lithuanian history that contained not only profound lessons for the generations of tomorrow but also helped to explain much of contemporary Baltic culture, politics and social structures.

I returned to the main road and to where I thought the bus would stop and take me to Druskininkai; common sense dictated that it would be roughly opposite to where I had been dropped off a short while earlier. So it was a little surprising—not to mention frustrating—when I saw the bus come into view from the side road into Grūtas village and, instead of turning right onto the main road, simply carry straight on and down a small side track running next to the first little lake I had admired earlier. So I now faced a quandary: I could stand around waiting for the next one in the hope that I would now be waiting in the right place, or I could hike for a couple of hours back into town. Given that I'd just spent a similar amount of time to that viewing the wonders of the park my tired legs quickly protested against any consideration of the latter.

Fortunately I was in luck: barely five minutes after sticking my thumb out a car, hesitant at first, eventually slowed and pulled over to the side of the road. I quickly jogged the short distance from where I had been standing—lest the driver have a sudden change of heart—and popped my head through the wound-down passenger window: "Druskininkai?" I asked, slightly breathless at the unexpected exertion. A simple nod and I jumped in.

The driver—a middle-aged man, probably about fifty or so—didn't speak much English, but by a combination of improvised sign language and the odd recognisable word we had a short but enjoyable drive back into town. I managed to work out that he was a lorry driver by trade, currently at home between jobs, and that he had hauled trucks all over Europe. "London, good!" he beamed, alarmingly taking both hands off the wheel to signal a double thumbs-up of approval.

Just slightly farther down the road we passed a turn signposted for Belarus, which from Druskininkai is only around five miles away. Indeed, the Vilnius-Druskininkai railway line was immensely popular in Soviet times, bringing health-seekers in their droves to take to the curative waters, but now the town's station lies disused and empty since the line runs through a short but bureaucratically significant section of Belarus. I asked the man, who had travelled all over the continent and beyond, whether he had ever been there. He shook his head as if to say "No, never." It was as if Belarus were another world entirely.

The journey from Vilnius to where Lithuania meets the Baltic is a long and lonely one, across a featureless and seemingly endless swathe of alternating grassland and forest. This is part of the vast European Plain, the lowland that stretches all the way from the Barents Sea in the frozen north to the Black Sea in the south and encompasses virtually all of north-eastern Europe. Fortunately the bus was a comfortable one, and I enjoyed plunging in and out of a novel I'd picked up at a hostel in the capital in between staring out at a landscape that made me feel insignificantly small in its vastness.

The road, a busy dual-carriageway, cuts directly through the very heart of the country like a great backbone, connecting Lithuania's three largest cities. As we sped past Kaunas it occurred to me that had we been travelling in the mid-1930s we would have just crossed over an international boundary.

Lithuania's attempts to build a modern and democratic nation rising Phoenix-like from the ashes of the Great War were short-lived. Relations with Poland—whose seizure of Vilnius was never accepted by the Lithuanian government—soured right from the start, and when a left-wing government signed a treaty of friendship with the Soviet Union in 1926 it was a step too far for President Antanas Smetona, who suspended parliament and introduced an increasingly authoritarian regime (with himself at the helm) that would last almost until the ending of independence some fifteen years later. Distrustful of its larger neighbours, and having attracted the ire of the Weimar Republic with its own unilateral seizure of the German-speaking port city of Memel (now known as Klaipėda) in 1923, Lithuania found itself increasingly to be the most isolated and inward-looking of the Baltics; even the 1934 signing of the "Baltic Entente" with its two northern neighbours did little to bring it in from the diplomatic cold.

It was to Klaipėda that I was headed. This city has been coveted by many regional powers throughout the ages, primarily due to its strategic ice-free location at the entrance to the Akmena-Danė River: at various times the port has been controlled by the Teutonic Knights, Prussia, the German Empire and, at the end of the First World War, by an allied occupation force primarily consisting of French troops pending a final decision on its status by the League of Nations.

It was in this febrile atmosphere that the Lithuanian authorities saw the opportunity to avenge the loss of Vilnius and to unite the Prussian Lithuanian minority—the Lietuvninkai—with the motherland. In January of 1923 a revolt staged by nationalists established within the Klaipėda Region (or Memelland) a pro-Lithuanian admin-istration in the city, a fait accompli formally recognised by the League a month later.

A humiliated Germany was forced to accept, but it refused to forget. So it was no surprise when, in March of 1939, the Nazi regime issued an ultimatum demanding that the Lithuanians give up the city and its hinterland upon threat of immediate invasion. None of the signato-ries of the 1924 Klaipėda Convention—which had guar-anteed Lithuanian sovereignty in the area—offered any assistance, thus leaving Lithuania with no option but to relinquish the region in what was Germany's last territo-rial acquisition before its invasion of Poland and the start of World War II several months later. Such was the glee with which Memel had been retaken that the Führer him-self turned up to mark the occasion.

This back-and-forth battle for the cultural domination of Klaipėda ended as the Soviet Red Army pushed back the

Nazi forces during the inexorable march towards Berlin, with the town's ethnic German population fleeing en masse. For much of the ensuing Soviet period Klaipėda's sensitive role as a major port rendered it largely off-limits to foreigners, a fact that has apparently done little to dampen its contemporary reputation as one of Lithuania's most accessible and welcoming cities.

I had arranged another couchsurf, this time with two women a couple of years younger than me who shared a flat on the opposite side of town from the modern station that our bus gently glided into after its epic trans-country trek. There had been a bit of confusion over exactly where it was I would meet them: rather than simply giving me their address—a piece of information vastly preferable to all else—I had a set of half-garbled directions that didn't entirely make sense. Perhaps it was the euphoria that comes with arriving in a new city, but I was feeling content and confident; after mooching outside a café for a few minutes in a none-too-subtle effort to sponge their wireless internet, I set off confidently in what I presumed to be the right direction.

The walk took me through the very centre of Klaipėda, a pleasant stroll that afforded a perfect little taste of what I might expect from my latest base. The streets were clean and lined with avenues of trees, and my wish to see what remained of the city's German heritage was amply rewarded with the sight of the marvellous post office, a red-brick Gothic masterpiece built in the late nineteenth century.

I eventually managed to find the place I was looking for, the result of a fortunate mixture of accident and design: it was a block of flats just opposite a statue that was situated on a suspiciously large and elaborate base that could only mean that it had once housed a mighty Lenin. I was early, so I found a comfy metal bench and tucked into a couple of sandwiches that had somehow survived the bus journey intact while I waited for Kristina. After a short while I saw a figure who looked vaguely familiar glide into view on the other side of the street, so I hastily dusted off the crumbs and made my way over.

It was indeed my hostess; she had been the one who had accepted my request for a place to stay with enthusiasm and who now greeted me with a smile and a kiss on the cheek that made my offer of a handshake seem stuffily British. "It's nice to meet you!" she beamed. "How was the journey?"

We made small talk as we wandered back to her place. Kristina had been at work; it had been a busy day, she told me, and she was glad to have finished. "And you will like my flatmates, they are really friendly people and they like having guests. Although one of them doesn't speak any English."

Kristina lived in a Soviet-era block of flats of the sort that were by now almost comforting in their familiarity. We walked up a couple of flights of stairs and then waited patiently as a couple of turns of the key opened the customary metal outer door, and then we were in.

Kristina's long-term housemate was named Klaudija, a girl with long blond hair that made her look—perhaps fittingly for what was once Prussian territory—a little bit Germanic, a fact partially explained by Klaudija's birth in what was then East Germany to a mixed German-Lithuanian couple. Making up the trio was Klaudija's sister, a younger girl who was the non-English speaker and who seemed to be in a constant state of embarrassment whenever we bumped into each other. I liked them all right from the start, and after dumping my bags in the spare room—the fourth housemate had only recently moved out—I joined them for drinks and pleasantries and to discuss the plan of action for the remainder of the evening: despite the long drive I was feeling surprisingly fresh.

"Sure, it would be nice to show you some of the city" said Kristina, sipping from a steaming cup of fruit tea. "But, er, I think Klaudija won't be joining us this evening! Will you, Klaudija?" Klaudija blushed at Kristina's teasing, and gave her a gentle push on the shoulder in a futile effort to halt her gossiping. But it was to no avail: "She has a date tonight!"

After Kristina got changed and I'd had the chance to freshen up we sauntered back into town. It was quieter now as the long light of an early summer evening basked us in a warm and mellow glow, and our meanderings took us into the cobbled gridiron streets of the Old Town.

Klaipėda is, as the locals like to remind the rest of the country, the oldest city in Lithuania, having been first mentioned in the Chronicles of Memelburg in 1252. For centuries it continued to prosper as a thoroughly German outpost of the Hanseatic League, trading with the rest of Northern Europe and serving as a gateway to its rich forests and amber deposits—almost all of the world's amber is sourced in the Baltic. And whilst much of the settlement was badly damaged in World War II we could still see traces of German history all over town, from a couple of half-timber-style (or *fachwerk*) edifices now home to hip-looking bars and restaurants to more of the red-brick civic buildings constructed in modest imitation of the city's post office. Some admittedly scruffy post-war restoration work had failed to dent what was on the whole a welcoming assemblage.

The focal point is Theatre Square, named after the ornate neoclassical edifice that stands on its northern flank. It was from the theatre's balcony that, in 1939, Adolf Hitler announce to rapturous crowds that Memel was once again German. Today it's a pleasant space replete with stalls selling assorted jewellery and trinkets to passing tourists; I picked up a small fridge magnet emblazoned with one of Klaipėda's more famous residents, the statue of "Anna" that stands astride a small fountain in front of the theatre. Anna was a famous pre-war monument commemorating the seventeenth-century German poet Simon Dach, who was born in the city and who taught in nearby Königsberg (modern-day Kaliningrad). Anna is the eponymous heroine from his folksong "Ännchen von Tharau," based on a real-life woman whom Dach reportedly fell in love with at first sight but who was tragically engaged to another man. Her current incarnation only dates from 1990, the original statue having been lost—like so many other cultural artefacts—during the Second World War. A small photo exhibition just behind the statue gave a further flavour of what historic Memel was once like.

It was soon apparent from our short walk that Klaipėda is a true patron of public arts, for festooned all over the city are statues ranging from the sublime to the fanciful, from mysterious to abstract. Almost every corner we turned seemed to bring us to another creation; there was the cat with the human face, the eerie ghost rising up from the depths of the Danė River and the chimney sweep sitting—appropriately enough—on top of a chimney.

My personal favourite, however, was "Stebuklingas Peliukas" (the "Magical Mouse"), a tiny little golden rodent sitting on his hind legs with a curious little smile on his face. "You should whisper something important to you into his ear," said Kristina softly. "It will bring you luck."

Kristina was a nice girl, with an infectious laugh and a pleasing smile that made for refreshingly welcome company. Her bright green eyes would flash as we walked and talked, the sunlight glinting off her long hair and forming a perfect frame in the half-light. And yet I could detect a certain sadness in her voice, like some dark thought casting a shadow that would manifest out of the corner of my eye and yet disappear completely whenever I looked at her directly, as if it had never been. It brought to mind the game of "grandmother's footsteps," where children try to catch friends creeping up on them, only to find them standing as still at statues whenever they turn around.

At the docks—next to a statue of a half-naked boy waving forlornly out to sea, a sailor's hat clasped in his hand—we stared out over cold waters to forested Neringa on the opposite shore. This thin sliver of land is the very northern tip of the great Curonian Spit that begins near Kaliningrad and ends here sixty miles later. Its presence almost within touching distance was equal parts invigorating and alluring, a strange and enticing world barely a stone's throw away that ached to be explored. But Neringa would have to wait, for there were more urgent matters to be attended to. "Let's get something to eat," suggested Kristina to what was an eagerly receptive audience.

We chose a place not far from the docks, near the centre of town—a cosy establishment located in a bigger building of what I reckoned to be either of pre-war German construction or in a style imitating that of the older Memel. We took a table for two, ordered something unhealthily satisfying (pizza and soft drink each), and passed some more pleasantries as we waited patiently—until, that is, a young woman from another table crept up behind Kristina and tapped her on the shoulder with a broad smirk on her face. From Kristina's reaction of hugs and shrieks of laughter I gathered that this was most likely an old and very good friend.

So instead of eating *à deux* we were now an integral part of a big group of lively Lithuanians. Kristina didn't know them all—they were colleagues of the friend whom it transpired Kristina had gone to school with—but we were quickly introduced. I found myself sitting next to a girl named Ruta, who in Klaipėda's small world also happened to be a friend of Klaudija's. "I hear she has a date tonight!" she joked.

We spoke and ate in a mixture of Lithuanian and English, a young population startlingly comfortable in its bilingualism. Ruta asked me how I knew Kristina and how I came to be in Klaipėda. I explained about the study and the couchsurfing, and Ruta seemed intrigued. "I set up a profile a while ago" she said, "but I never used it yet. I always wondered what it would be like, but"—she paused for a moment—"I guess I would be a bit nervous about meeting someone new that I didn't know. But you seem nice. How long will you stay in Klaipėda?"

This was a good question. Klaudija and Kristina were only able to take me in for the night; it was nearly the weekend and both of them would soon be away. I wasn't quite sure what I was going to do—perhaps find another host in town or head back to Kaunas for some more high larks with Arminas, Rasa and Vytis, the trio of students who had kindly given me an open invitation to return whenever I was in the area.

"Well, perhaps I could take you," offered Ruta. "I don't have many plans this weekend. As long as you're comfortable sleeping on a couch, because I don't have extra bed. But it's a nice couch and you'd be very welcome. I promise."

I relayed this good news to Kristina as we trekked back home in the sultry summer night, but she seemed distracted. "Oh, I think she is probably a nice girl," she said a little absentmindedly. "But I don't really know her all that well. She's Klaudija's friend. I'm sure you'll have a nice time, though."

I felt extremely happy. I had only been in Klaipėda a short time and I'd already met a dozen people, swapped numbers and email addresses with several new friends, and found a place to stay in what was quickly becoming one of my favourite towns in the Baltics. And it wasn't just about spending this time with good company, either; couchsurfing had already proved itself to be by far the best way to truly understand what life as a local is really like. I felt very lucky indeed.

"So what will you be doing this weekend?" I asked Kristina as we climbed the stairs to the door of her apartment.

She stopped and, for the first time, looked me straight in the eye. "I will be moving to my boyfriend's town, and soon we'll be starting our preparations to get married."

There wasn't even a hint of a smile on her lips.

CHAPTER 12

The City by the Sea

* * *

I JUMPED WITH A START as the car screeched to a halt next to me with a couple of beeps of its horn. I could see a figure waving frantically from the driver's seat, beckoning me over and opening up the passenger door as I approached: it was Ruta, all smiles and cheers. "Hey!" she exclaimed as I threw my bag onto the back seat and clambered in. "It's good to see you!"

It was good to see her, too. Before arriving once more back in Klaipėda I had indeed gone back to Kaunas the previous night, where I'd met up with a Lithuanian-based colleague of the Leeds-based credit reference agency I had once had the misfortune to work for. A few months prior to my Baltic adventure the company had opened an office in Kaunas, ostensibly because of the scarcity of specific skills back in the UK that appeared to have been abundant in the fourth-largest city in the Baltics—a notion the more cynical of us might have dismissed in favour of the cheaper labour that Lithuania was able to provide. Whatever the reality of the matter, it would be fair to say that the small cohort of Lithuanians who were sent over to train with us for a couple of months were all intelligent, highly motivated and enthusiastic to a fault: qualities that the rest of us had been sorely lacking for some time. Vitalija was the senior of those new colleagues, and I enjoyed a quick hour sipping tea at an Old Town café as she chain-smoked her way through half a packet of cigarettes. It was a phenomenon I'd noticed back in Yorkshire, where she had quickly become legendary for the number of smoking breaks she would take during the day. At least she was consistent in her habits.

My intended stay with Arminas and company didn't quite pan out the way I'd planned, either; all three turned out to be away, but they still came up trumps by very kindly giving me the contact details of a sympathetic friend who lived just around the corner from their flat. So after I bid farewell to Vitalija—a somewhat conspiratorial affair that took place down a side street so that her husband wouldn't ask what she was doing socialising with another man—I made my way to a new home for the night that was comfortable, clean and perhaps best of all didn't have a vomiting cat in residence.

And now, the following lunchtime, I was standing near Klaipėda's bus station waiting for Ruta when she suddenly appeared as if by magic. It hadn't been the best start to my arrival—I had been hassled by a patience-sapping and heavily intoxicated man who spoke in slurred Lithuanian inside the station, and I also managed to break a clip on my bag—but this was quickly forgotten as I felt myself melt in her perfect white smile. A quick hug to further cement this rapidly spiralling infatuation and we were off.

Ruta drove fast, and after a few short and occasionally hair-raising minutes we parked ourselves in a small street near one of Klaipėda's iconic landmarks: the *Meridianas*, a large wooden sailing ship moored permanently in the centre of town. We got out and walked a short distance over cobbles until we got to our first destination of the day, a trendy café *cum* art gallery on the edge of Klaipėda's Old Town situated in a beautiful pale-yellow building overlooking the river.

Ruta was an estate agent by trade who kept herself busy during the week showcasing apartments to families and couples and other middle-class types attracted to Klaipėda's coastal location and relatively benign climate. Business seemed to be doing very well, which was an indication of the booming local economy that is now most notably symbolised by the two towering office blocks forming the letters *K* and *D* that loom above the New Town.

On the weekends Ruta would amuse herself in other ways; here at the café she volunteered in a number of positions that seemed to include looking after the finances and various other bits of office administration, as well as serving up a mean coffee. "It's a community-led project," she explained as I took in the artworks on the wall. "They're all made by local artists here in Klaipėda. Mostly art students. You can buy one if you like."

It was a tempting offer. Some of the smaller paintings were actually rather good, but instead I had to make do with a fancy drink called a chai latte that, despite my initial scepticism, wasn't all that bad. It just seemed sad that such a nice place was so conspicuously empty of customers.

"Yes, it's a problem," confided Ruta after she had finished whatever it was that she had needed to do. "The place is losing money but the owner is hoping that business will pick up. I hope it does, because he is a young guy and it would be nice if it succeeded. But already several months have passed and it's not getting any busier." She didn't sound confident.

Ruta had seemed pleased when I told her why I was in Lithuania, as if someone taking an interest in the recent history of the Baltics was an unusual thing: a phenomenon that was still not yet common beyond this small corner of northeast Europe. So now we were walking around parts of the city that I'd not seen in my earlier tour with Kristina. "There is something I want to show you," she whispered in my ear, in a way that thrilled me more than it should have.

Not far from the café, on the other side of the Danė, was a striking memorial in the shape of an arch situated at the entrance to a tree-filled park. It struck me that in some ways the arch resembled one of those games of hangman you might play on a long car journey: the upright and crosspiece were made of a grey-coloured stone whilst a red-coloured column seemingly propped up the rest of the construction. This monument, it transpired, symbolised the reunification of Lithuania Minor with the rest of the country after the Second World War. At the top I could make out the inscription *Esame Viena Tauta, Viena Žemė, Viena Lietuva.* I asked Ruta what it meant. "'One People, One Land, One Lithuania'" she intoned. The red column was Klaipėda: take it away from Lithuania and the whole edifice would come crashing down. I wondered if the roughly 20 per cent of the city's inhabitants who identified themselves as ethnic Russians would necessarily agree with its sentiments.

I asked Ruta about this as we carried on our way. Her response was interesting; yes, she believed that independence had not just been a good thing for Lithuania but was indeed the natural and morally correct state of affairs. Ruta's generation were enjoying greater freedoms than their parents: they could travel, live and work abroad, voice their opinions more freely, were more affluent, and had more on which to spend their earnings. This was no great surprise. But then Ruta started to talk about the strident nationalism of the new Lithuanian state and how this was not always worthy of celebration, that it could sometimes be overbearing and suffocating. It was similar to what I'd heard from Leonidas: a narrative that could not be questioned. Any attempt to do so was deemed unpatriotic or at worse subversive, part and parcel of the existential threat posed by the Russian giant poised and ready at the nation's borders.

We reached another green space, home to the wonderfully whimsical Martynas Mažvydas Sculpture Park. Built on the site of a former cemetery that had been cleared by the Soviets, around a hundred or so statues lay dotted among the trees. They all seemed to date from the last couple of decades or so prior to independence, and some were even interactive. I particularly liked the riding saddle supported by a single, thick hooved horse's leg; as I posed precariously on this unusual seat a toddler looked on enviously, impatiently awaiting his turn. Then there was the stylised cyclist, the outlandish furniture, the stone cat, and the bull with an anvil perched on his back. I noticed that many of them were in the same bicoloured red-and-grey as the reunification arch.

Mažvydas, incidentally, was the author of the first book—the *Catechism*—printed in the Lithuanian language. Born not far from Klaipėda and raised in Vilnius, given the high regard he is now held within Lithuania it is somewhat ironic that Mažvydas was persecuted for his Protestant leanings and was forced to seek shelter in Prussian Königsberg, where his book was published in 1547.

Also interesting is the fact that all Lithuanian-language publications printed in the Latin alphabet were banned within the Russian Empire from 1864 until the lifting of the restriction forty years later. This, the so-called Press Ban, was a response to the January Uprising of a year before and was an attempt to promote a Russification of the Lithuanian people whilst simultaneously combatting Polish influence. Lithuanian publications printed in Cyrillic were encouraged, and the printing, importation, possession and distribution of Latin-script texts became illegal. The policy failed completely; books and periodicals published in Prussia and the United States were smuggled into Lithuania by book smugglers—the *knygnešiai*—and the ban inadvertently created an organised and well-motivated opposition to Russian rule and culture. It's even been suggested that without the ban and the resultant resistance Lithuanian language and culture would have slipped into oblivion and there would be no modern Lithuanian state.

And Lithuanian is unusual. Along with Latvian it's one of only two surviving languages of the Baltic language family, a group of immense interest to linguists as it retains many archaic features believed to have been present in the early stages of the Proto-Indo-European language: the common ancestor of the modern Indo-European languages that dominate much of the world's surface. Having changed relatively little over its history, Lithuanian is said to be the most conservative living Indo-European language.

At the edge of the sculpture park was the real reason for our visit. I could see what we were looking for before we had reached it: a huge sword dangling downwards between two giant concrete pillars that themselves were joined near the base. Close by were three giant soldiers of the Red Army, complete with rifles and chisel-like jaw lines.

Lining the memorial were lists of names, all in Cyrillic. This was Klaipėda's Soviet war memorial, dedicated to those who lost their lives in the Great Patriotic War.

In front of the sword and the soldiers was a large open space covered with small square concrete slabs. It was clearly intended for large gatherings but on this balmy weekend we pretty much had the place to ourselves. As we stared up at the silent sentinels staring defiantly into the distance Ruta grabbed my arm and told me that as a child she had found them scary. "And I still do" she confided.

The likely response may have been obvious but I had to ask. "Do you feel any sort of connection with this place? I mean, would you ever want to come here on May Ninth to remember the war?" She almost seemed bemused by the question.

"Only the old people come here," she said. "*Russians.*"

Just as in Tartu I was struggling to find something smart to wear. Ever since I'd hitchhiked around Ireland as a student I'd subscribed to the travel-light school of thought; it turned out that heavy bags don't make for fun companions, particularly when stranded on a damp and drizzly County Mayo roadside in September. The downside to this strategy is that there is a direct correlation between bag size and sartorial variety, which can make formal social situations particularly challenging.

"I don't have any smart shoes" I complained as I tried to iron six-week-old creases from the single shirt I'd managed to coax from the depths of my pack. "I hope that won't be a problem."

"It should be fine," smiled Ruta as she shot past and into the bathroom. "I don't think they will mind too much: it's not a nightclub or anything like that."

We'd spent an agreeable afternoon cycling around the forests that surrounded Ruta's apartment block. She lived on the northern edge of the city, on the top floor, and the view from the small terrace was absolutely stunning: forests that seemed to stretch right to the horizon, as far as the eye could see. It was an illusion, of course; somewhere beyond that tree line was the cold, deep Baltic Sea.

This proximity was obvious as we had made our way on the numerous paths that snaked their way through the trees, the small mounds of sandy soil covering the roots and vegetation belying our coastal location. It was an enviable facility for local residents; just a short stroll and it felt like we'd entered another world entirely, where the sounds and smells of the city seemed far, far away. Ruta had even shown me a short video clip of two huge elk-like creatures emerging from the trees only a few yards from her front door.

Ruta's apartment was different to those I'd stayed in previously. This was no run-down Khrushchyovka; this was a clean, modern flat that felt so new that I imagined I could smell the paint drying on the walls. "It's only a couple of years old" confirmed Ruta as I wandered around, marvelling at its size. "I managed to find it because of my job. I guess it can be lucky working with property."

Ruta had not lived there long. Previously she had been with her parents, who lived only a short distance away. But here she was happy: "I have my freedom and I can visit my parents whenever I want. Which is good, because my father"—here she broke off for a second—"is not well at the moment."

That evening we were going to a fashion show of all places: exactly the sort of locale that might not appreciate a shoddily dressed attendee—indeed, only the previous night a burly bouncer had turned me away from a bar for wearing trainers. One of Ruta's friends was a fashion-design student and some of his work would be featured; he had very kindly extended an invitation to both of us. "I'm serious, don't worry" Ruta laughed as she sauntered past draped in only a towel, a smaller one wrapped carefully around her head. "It's a charity event, part of an arts festival that's been going on all week. They won't mind if you're a bit scruffy. I promise."

We drove into the city and left the car not far from the Soviet memorial. A short walk later and we were at the venue, a large warehouse down by the docks with a small queue waiting patiently outside. A young doorman checked our tickets and waved us inside, into a big hall with a raised catwalk and plastic chairs lining either side. It was already busy, so it took us a little while to find two adjoining seats that weren't already occupied or being saved for someone else. Presently we met with success; it wasn't front-row seating, but the view still promised to be a good one. Yet despite this I was feeling a little apprehensive, partly because I'd never been particularly interested in fashion and had always thought of such shows as being on the wrong side of pretentious. At least it's dark, I thought; this way they won't see my decidedly unfashionable footwear.

The lights went out completely, and moody music slowly drifted softly over the stage. A spotlight lit up a dark curtain and a figure appeared from behind it, moving slowly and purposefully towards the centre. Then another appeared, and another, all dressed in an eye-catching array of clothes modelled on some strange sort of bird. They wore blues and blacks and reds; rich, dark colours that on their own wouldn't have commanded much attention and yet they complemented one another wonderfully. This wasn't what I was expecting at all, for this was no mere strut down the catwalk. This was something altogether more poetic, more artistic: a choreographed dance of subtle beauty that was curious and captivating all at the same time.

Further acts followed, including some standard strutting with models wearing a range of clothing ranging from the sublime to the ridiculous: some practical, some purely conceptual. But others were more like the opening sequence: moving dance ensembles that somehow seemed more like art than fashion. Despite my initial hesitation I found that I was having a wonderful time.

Afterward Ruta and I found her friend; it transpired that he had masterminded the first arrangement, as well as featuring in quite a few of the costumes that appeared later on in the show. Ruta had pointed him out during one such procession, and I thought I had spotted him several times afterwards. "It was so crazy backstage!" he confirmed as we made our way to Ruta's car. "But it was really fun. I'm so glad you were able to make it."

The night was not yet over. We drove through the now-dark streets of Klaipėda to a residential area in a part of the city I'd not been to before. These apartments looked modern, too; indeed, the city really felt like a place that was developing at a greater speed than the rest of the country: evidence once more of a galvanised and confident local economy. But we were not here to marvel at this dynamism, for there were far more serious matters afoot: the Eurovision Song Content.

A couple of flights of stairs and a quick knock at a door and we were inside another spacious apartment; unlike Ruta's place, however, this one was packed full of Lithuanians: over a dozen men and women, all under the age of thirty or so. The host was the one who answered the door: "Welcome!" she beamed as she motioned us in, greeting us all with a kiss on each cheek. "It's already started. Quick, get yourself a drink, and there's plenty of food, too."

Fortunately we hadn't missed much. We all sat in front of a large TV screen on whatever we could find; the lucky ones had the sofa, others chairs and stools, whilst the slower among us had to make do with the floor. I grabbed a few snacks and found a comfy-looking spot next to Ruta, making the most of this excuse for closer proximity.

A few countries had already come and gone, and when we arrived the flat had been suffused with a jovial, carnival-like atmosphere. But as Lithuania's act kicked in this instantly changed: silence descended upon the crowd and the once-boisterous attendees suddenly adopted a hushed air of respect. This was serious stuff indeed, and not at all to be scoffed at: I was roundly chastised in both word and scowl by several members of the party when I dared whisper a question to my companion. Even Ruta wasn't smiling any more.

I was genuinely finding it hard to see what all the fuss was about. I'd never been much of a fan of Eurovision; all that mundane music and glitzy camp simply didn't do it for me, Britain's perennial "nil points" notwithstanding. And yet I was about to witness a curious confirmation of a widely held suspicion that not all was right with the voting system this glorified karaoke competition employed.

The excitement in the room was palpable as the Lithuanian entry completed his routine to claps and cheers and nods of approval from his compatriots both in the studio audience and here in this packed room in Klaipėda. As the next country limbered up on the screen the gentle hubbub of before gradually returned to the room, like a long, slow exhale following three minutes of tensely held breath.

The general consensus, it seemed, was that their boy had done well: perhaps not enough to win the competition outright, but certainly enough to be in contention. So as the contest entered the stage in which each individual country scores its peers the excitement began to mount once again. And for good reason, for it turned out that my companions were able to predict with uncanny accuracy how other nations would rate Lithuania's entry. "Brilliant—it's Georgia," remarked a young man sitting on the other side of Ruta as he nodded approvingly. "They will give us the full mark." When Georgia duly did, I had to ask him why. "Oh, they've always given us do since we supported them in their war against Russia." The casual way that he offered this explanation suggested that this was not a practice without precedent; the notion that acts might be scored on their actual ability rather than a favourable geopolitical relationship was an amusing yet thoroughly naive concept. Geopolitics seemed to be the determining factor; as if to illustrate the point, the room expressed near-outrage when Latvia failed to deliver a decent score, which everyone deemed to be a calculated and deliberate insult. Surprising, perhaps, given that relations between the Baltic states are generally considered to be very good.

Lithuania finished in upper-mid table, a result my companions perceived to be a disappointment. The UK, meanwhile, predictably foundered near the bottom. "Don't worry" sympathised a grinning Ruta as I pretended to be distraught. "It's always this way. The UK will never win Eurovision." I didn't doubt her words for a second.

I spent a delightful few days in Ruta's company: we explored more of the forests that surrounded her home, swapped stories over coffees and art at her volunteer café, and went to the cinema to watch the latest Hollywood offering. This was a surprisingly straightforward affair for me, since new releases are nearly always subtitled, there simply not being enough Lithuanian speakers to merit dubbed translations. We even went to Palanga with several of her friends, the seaside resort a short distance up the coast where Lithuanians love to come to enjoy warm summer evenings on the sandy shore. It has a rickety wooden pier stretching far out to sea, and we walked with linked arms as the setting sun set the sky a fiery red. I came to the realisation that I never wanted this moment to end, and thoughts of Mari had been all but banished in my mind.

But sadly, and inexorably, I came to the realisation that my time in Klaipėda was slowly drawing to a close. In Ruta's apartment I had made my home on her sofa in a spare room and, as much as I felt myself becoming increasingly besotted, I could not impose myself indefinitely on her time. She was a busy girl, with numerous commitments, and the one thing that seemed worse than leaving her was to commit the crime of outstaying my welcome.

So, with a heavy heart, it was time to pack my things and bid her farewell. "Thank you for a lovely visit; it was very nice to meet you," she smiled as I prepared to board my bus. "And of course, you know you are welcome back anytime you like. Just send me a message and I'll come pick you up. Safe travels."

As I waved farewell I couldn't help but wondering if she knew just how much I wanted to take her up on the offer.

CHAPTER 13

Behind Bars

* * *

THE BOY COULDN'T HAVE BEEN any older than three or four, and yet there he was aimlessly wandering around in the middle of the road. It was mid-morning and already busy with cars, and although the first couple of vehicles successfully swerved in time to avoid him it seemed only a matter of moments before something much more deadly would happen. So without a pause I raced over, scooped him up in my arms, and dashed for the safety of the pavement.

He was young—on inspection perhaps even closer to two—and he looked around blankly as he ignored my feeble attempts to communicate. I attempted in vain to spot a parent or other adult who might know where the child had come from, but there wasn't a soul to be seen. Of course there was no question that I could simply leave him at the side of the road, so I hesitantly shuffled back over to the entrance of the hostel that I'd left just moments before and climbed the stairs to the first floor with the mysterious little boy cradled in my arms.

It didn't take me long to find Inga, the young woman who was running the property, and she laughed a little as I explained to her the somewhat surreal series of events that had just taken place. "I think I recognise him," she said as she took the boy from me. "He belongs to the family downstairs. I'll take him to them; I'm sure they will be pleased to see him. Won't they, my beautiful?" she whispered as she carried him back in the direction I'd just come, presumably to the flat that took up the ground floor of the building we were currently standing in.

It was a strange start to the day. I'd arrived in Liepāja the afternoon before, emerging blinking from a nearly empty bus into a bright sun set in a sky of pure blue. Something about that kind of light can make even the drabbest of places seem to sparkle, and as I trekked in the direction of the centre of town I was pleasantly surprised by what I saw: all tree-lined avenues and cobbled streets, not at all what I was expecting from an industrial port city that was once the temporary home of Russia's mighty Baltic Fleet. I was immediately charmed.

The journey to Liepāja had been smooth, if uneventful, and I noted as we sped past the sign marking the Latvian border with Lithuania the now-empty buildings that once would have housed police and guards. We stopped off for a short break to let the driver have a smoke in a small town where several of the passengers alighted, and by the time we reached Latvia's third-largest city only myself and one other passenger remained on board. And now here I was, rescuing children and feeling distinctly unwell.

It had started in the evening of the same day I'd arrived. I had found the hostel easily enough; it was in the Old Town, not far from the sea and, just like the bus earlier in the morning, it seemed practically deserted. Inside was the proprietor—the young woman whom I guessed to be in her mid-twenties or thereabouts—and an American backpacker who seemed to be partway through a never-ending world tour, and that was about it. But instead of wanting to dump my things and head straight off in the direction of the beach I quickly realised that I wasn't feeling all that great. My head was beginning to hurt more and more and I sensed in the pit of my stomach that I was feeling increasingly nauseated: not only that, my lower back was so sore that any change from a vertical posture resulted in agonising spasms shooting up and down my spine. In short, I felt like crap. This was new territory for me, for I'd always prided myself on having a rock-solid constitution; I couldn't remember the last time I'd taken a genuine sick day from work and I always generally felt okay. Liepāja seemed to have other plans for me though, so I ended up spending the afternoon and evening either curled up in bed or bumming around the hostel feeling ever-so-sorry for myself.

Luckily, as hostels go, this one was actually rather nice—there was a shop close by for comfort food and the kitchen was well stocked with equipment, and the place also had a computer that I was able to entertain myself with during some of my more lucid moments. I also got chatting with Inga, who, between chasing after her bratty and extremely naughty five-year-old son, would do odd jobs around the hostel—not that there was a great deal to do given the number of people staying there. She seemed bored and dissatisfied, and confided in me as such as she openly pined for the bright lights of Riga. As we sat together watching online videos of nothing in particular she asked me if I had any hobbies. I confirmed that I did, listing a number of interests and mentioning that I had once been a keen rugby player. "And dancing, do you like it?" she asked, to which I shook my head and confessed that I possessed the proverbial two left feet. "I have just started this new type of dance here in Liepāja; it's hard, but I really like it so far. Here, let me show you."

She found a clip of two men engaging in capoeira, the gracefully athletic Brazilian dance that is more akin to a noncontact martial art than something you might do down at the local discotheque. When performed well it's absolutely mesmerising, the co-ordinated kicks and backflips of the participants whirling together in perfect harmony. It takes skill, stamina and acrobatic flair, and is both technically and physically extremely difficult. "You're doing this?" I asked, somewhat impressed and also curious as to how an iconic piece of Brazilian culture had a participative presence here on Latvia's west coast.

"Well, I've only just started it," she confessed with a smile. "It's hard but I enjoy it. My friend invited me, but the man who runs it is a nigger from Brazil. Do you like niggers?"

My jaw almost hit the floor. I couldn't quite believe my ears: Did she really just use this outmoded and offensive word?

"I can't stand them," she went on, oblivious to my shock. "And the guy who runs the class, this nigger seems okay but obviously I don't trust him. Do you have many niggers in England?"

Every use of the word made me squirm, like a sledge-hammer hitting my head over and over. It made me wince. It made me desperately uncomfortable. It was agonising.

"Um, well yes, there are a lot of black people in the UK" I mumbled, hoping she might note my lack of use of the N-word. "And many Asians and Europeans and Americans. It's a very diverse society, which generally makes us very tolerant of other cultures."

I was rapidly deciding that I didn't like Inga all that much. My suspicions had first been aroused when the subject of my Baltic project first cropped up in conversation: "Gypsies" was the pejorative term she used to describe Latvia's Russian speakers. "No one needs these people: Russia doesn't need them, Latvia doesn't need them." And now here she was bandying around a term that was so outdated and offensive that it hurt my ears just to hear it. She even shook her head as I tried to extol the virtues of multiplicity and tolerance: a diversity, I noted with some irony, that she was ready to take advantage of by partaking in a distinctly South American physical activity that had no obvious cultural connection to Latvia. To save argument I meekly let it drop. But at least this ugly interaction convinced me to get out of bed promptly the following morning, even though I was feeling worse than ever. And outspoken racists and child-rescuing endeavours aside, I actually had another good reason to be up: Karosta.

It was actually the American who really whetted my appetite. The previous evening, after the unfortunate incident with Inga, the man from New York had shown me a series of photos taken earlier that day of him dressed in Soviet-style army uniforms and clutching a replica Kalashnikov, otherwise commonly known as the AK-47. "You can do it at Karosta," he explained as I looked on enviously. "You just have to ask them. I'm telling you, man, they got tonnes of Soviet shit." Shit indeed. It sounded perfect.

Karosta—the name is a contraction of *kara osta*, meaning "naval port"—was actually the primary incentive for my visit to Liepāja. This exclusively Russian-speaking enclave a few miles to the north of Liepāja's centre has a fascinating history. Developed at great expense by the Tsarist authorities in the late nineteenth century to guard against potential German naval attack, the fortified port and gun batteries were never actually put to the test—at the onset of war in 1914 the Baltic Fleet sank ballast in the harbour and withdrew to Tallinn and Helsinki. But it was after the Second World War that Karosta really gained in importance; it was commandeered as a Soviet submarine base to become a self-contained garrison town entirely off-limits to locals and foreigners alike. And just like Daugavpils's fortress, a local population dependent on the base for employment has since been left stranded by the pulling out of the military machine it once served.

I got a bus up to the Kalpaks Bridge, an elegant green structure built sometime in the years leading up to the First World War that marks the southern entrance to Karosta. It's a particularly attractive marvel of engineering; a complex mechanism enables it to swing open to let boats and ships through in an operation that lasts around five minutes, although sadly it was stationary as I crossed over the broad canal that separates this "city within a city" from Liepāja proper.

I wasn't really sure what to expect. I'd picked up a leaflet in the hostel that enigmatically described the "brutal enchantment of Karosta," but as I wandered through the leafy streets dotted with apartment blocks I was impressed with how unthreatening a place it seemed. It was a glorious day, and life all around me was carrying on as normal: cats stalked one another through the bushes and women hung out washing as their children danced and played around their feet. It was actually rather pleasant and not at all intimidating, although the first sign that this was no ordinary place came from an unexpected source: with a chuckle I noted that many of the public waste bins were made from hollowed-out bombshells.

This self-contained city of contrasts was neatly illustrated as I turned a corner and almost walked straight into the large Cathedral of Saint Nicholas, a beautifully ornate edifice quite at odds with the Khrushchyovka surrounding it. Built in 1901 to serve the naval garrison installed by its namesake Tsar, the building later served as a sports hall, a cinema and a so-called red corner—a recreation and entertainment room—during the Soviet period. I learned that the interior of the central cupola had been bricked up to diminish the echoey acoustics so that the sailors could hear their films more clearly but today it acts once again as a functioning Orthodox church, its majestic onion domes calling the faithful of Karosta to prayer and contemplation.

I was beginning to learn that Karosta, unlike Daugavpils, is not a fortress of childlike imagination surrounded by high walls and cannons and ditches. Rather the old fabric of the original naval base reveals itself in much more subtle ways: wide, tree-lined boulevards adjoin cobbled streets and Soviet-era apartment blocks soon give way to quieter areas of older red-brick buildings, all in various states of repair—remnants from the original bout of construction. Some of these are particularly fine: the beautiful water tower, once supplying the entire port with drinking water and still in use (albeit using modern pumps) in the same capacity today, and the impressive Manege, a walled enclosure once used for competitions and performances by the base's cavalry and artillery horses. Art nouveau even made an appearance in the form of the Convention House, a grand but now sadly dilapidated building that once catered to the needs of the visiting Tsarist aristocracy. I tried to imagine the privileged fellows who once would have graced its halls and what they would think to see their once-majestic mansion slowly decaying in the salty air.

But I could not tarry, for Karosta also harbours a darker secret and it was to this that I was heading—and despite the headache and the nausea and the agonising back pain it was impossible not to feel an increasing sense of excitement.

Eventually I found the forbidding red-brick building that somehow seemed more sinister than the rest: the prison, a detention facility successively used to punish disorderly sailors, first by the Tsarist and then subsequently by the interwar Latvian and Soviet authorities. The last inmates only moved out in 1997 but somewhat ironically it actually started its life as a naval hospital. These days it serves a far less ominous purpose catering to tourists curious to see a slice of life that few would have relished experiencing for real.

The entrance was well signposted, and the omens were good; a military-style personnel carrier adorned with a Soviet star and a watchtower flanked the path to the front door, where inside I found a couple of staffers dressed in glorious militaristic uniforms. "Please, come with me," instructed a man of around forty after I'd paid for my ticket, "I will guide you around the prison."

My personal tour guide spoke an intermediate level of English, but he clearly enjoyed his job; throughout the gloomy corridors and grimy cells he would point out things of interest or recount the history of the prison, all the while giving me relative freedom to explore at my own pace. The graffiti scrawled on the walls by the last inmates seemed particularly poignant, while the tiny red cross hidden above the entrance hinted at the building's original purpose.

Upstairs couldn't have been more different. Here were the administrator's offices, a veritable shrine to Soviet rule: busts of Lenin and red flags framed rooms filled with twentieth-century kitsch that no doubt would have once been comfortingly familiar to the bureaucrats who ran the facility. I was only slightly disappointed that there wasn't an AK-47 or a spare Soviet officer's trench coat to be seen, but I was feeling so rough that I couldn't be bothered to ask.

Funnily enough it wasn't the first time I'd felt slight disappointment with my trip to Karosta. The prison is famous for its "Behind Bars" experience, where actors dressed up as prison guards frogmarch visitors around at gunpoint, bellowing orders and singing rousing Marxist songs as they might have done in the days of the USSR. To get the true full-on prison experience it's even possible to bed down for the night in the cells, with the guards on hand to ensure that none of the "inmates" are planning an escape. I'd contacted the prison a month in advance to find out if any English translation would be available during the time I was to be in Liepāja—Russian or Latvian is the norm—but the reply was in the negative. This was probably not a bad thing given my condition when I finally arrived, but it still felt like an opportunity missed.

"Behind Bars" is not the only event that the prison holds, as I found out whilst sipping a delicious hot chocolate in the cafeteria that once would have been the inmates' mess hall. I found a small brochure which detailed a range of interactive programmes that included such delights as a "Day in the Army," a "Day in the Detention Quarters" and the intriguing—if somewhat ambiguous-sounding—"Civil Defence Exercises." They even advertised stag events and birthday parties, but the one that appealed to me most was "Escape from the USSR," a team game taking place not at the prison itself but at nearby fortifications to the north of the main site. Here groups have to rescue a friend from under the noses of patrolling guards and attempt to reach a submarine that would facilitate their escape. It sounded like fantastic fun.

Karosta, and the events that it runs, is indicative of the growing popularity of Soviet-era sights right across the Baltics. For example, in the eastern part of Latvia (not far from the village of Līgatne) stands the Vidzeme Regional Rehabilitation Centre: once the holiday retreat of high-ranking members of the Soviet regime and also home to a top-secret complex of underground bunkers that was intended to serve as a shelter for the LSSR's top brass in the event of a nuclear war. The ninety-odd rooms, decorated with military maps and some of the earliest reel-to-reel computers to be produced in the Soviet Union, are now open to curious members of the public. And in Lithuania's Žemaitija National Park the Plokštinė missile base—a site that previously housed SS-4 medium-range ballistic missiles armed with two-megatonne nuclear warheads pointing directly at the cities of Western Europe—has now been converted into a Cold War Museum where visitors can gawp at one of the four existing silos. For tourists, at least, the Soviet Union has never been so accessible.

As I sipped my beverage it occurred to me that while the likes of Grūtas Park were controversial when they first opened it appeared that there was a growing acknowledgment of the Soviet period as an integral part of Baltic history, even as others continued to push the widespread "bury and forget" policy that had been in place since the realisation of independence. And whilst Karosta's light-hearted approach might not to be to the taste of all, it suggested that if plenty of Latvians were comfortable with this then perhaps the ghosts of the Soviet Union were being treated as the past of a former generation and not of the people in the here and now. Or maybe I had it all wrong: perhaps it was simply gallows humour, designed to detract from the collective trauma of the occupation, or perhaps political paradigms simply didn't matter when it came to making a quick buck. Whatever the reality, it made me wonder what the more solemn museums in Riga and elsewhere would make of it all.

As I slowly stepped out blinking into the sunlight, I realised that Karosta's commercialisation of its prison also had another significant benefit: that of preservation, both of the physical structure and of the memory of the events that took place there. It was a sharp contrast to Tallinn's Patarei, whose slow decay and potential loss certainly made for a far creepier visit but that also carried with it the very real danger of inducing a collective amnesia.

But then that's perhaps because Karosta is much more than a prison. It continues to be a living and breathing but also isolated community, a unique relic of Russia's— and later the Soviet Union's—dominance of this stretch of coast. And even now her military days are not quite over; as I crossed once more over the Kalpaks Bridge I could spy the modern facilities of the Baltic Navy Diving Training Centre on the shores of the canal, the only one of its kind in the region. In this very small corner of Latvia's westernmost province the Soviet legacy resolutely soldiers on.

CHAPTER 14

The Great Outdoors

∗　∗　∗

SIGULDA WAS, QUITE LITERALLY, A breath of fresh air. The town is situated in the heart of the scenic Gauja Valley, a beautifully forested area by local standards so full of lumps and bumps that Baltic Germans fancifully christened it the "Livonian Switzerland." It's barely an hour away from Riga and yet somehow it manages to feel like a different country entirely, and for many the region represents the very essence of Latvia: rural, bucolic and achingly beautiful.

I had come here to blow away the cobwebs of the mystery affliction that I had struggled with in Liepāja. I once again transferred through Riga, this time pausing only to admire a large map on an interior wall of the bus station that revealed just how far north we really were: the Latvian capital is almost on the same latitude as Aberdeen, with lofty Tallinn on a par with the likes of Shetland or Labrador on Canada's east coast. It had been a long way to come but now, as I savoured the view from Artists' Hill, I felt a like a person reborn. In one direction, forest stretched on either side of the gently flowing Gauja right to the horizon; in the other, turreted castles straight from the pages of a fairy-tale poked majestically through the canopy. The sun was shining and the sky was pure blue. Quite simply, it was heaven.

Unsurprisingly, I wasn't the first person to fall in love with Sigulda. Nationally important artists like Janis Rozentāls and Vilhelms Purvītis had come here to paint romantic landscapes—giving its most famous viewpoint its name in the process—and nearby caves were scored with the deeply etched graffiti of previous generations. Indeed, it first became popular with Saint Petersburg's well-to-do with the construction of the Riga-Valka railway in the mid-nineteenth century and has remained Latvia's most popular inland resort ever since. But today I was in luck, for there were no crowds; I pretty much had the place to myself.

It's easy to spend a lot of time in Sigulda simply wandering around, and that's exactly what I did; forested paths took me through an enchanted landscape of verdant hills and every now and then a break in the trees would offer another picturesque vista, another excuse to stop and pause awhile simply to drink it all in. I loved how the light would break through the trees in shafts of brightness, dancing through the leaves in an air that was as sweet as could be.

The town itself was also relatively unscathed by Soviet development and it reminded me a little of Druskininkai, in that it seemed like clearings had been made between the buildings for the trees to grow rather than the other way around. It gave it a wonderfully organic feel, and it made me think how nice it would be if all the world's cities were as close to nature as this. And there was history, too, with Sigulda Castle offering a brief respite (if such a thing were needed) from the beautiful surroundings. It was quiet almost to the extent of being deserted; a lone employee dressed in the garb of a medieval peasant slouched against a wall looking thoroughly bored. But it mattered not, for this well-presented Livonian fortress made for fine exploration.

So, too, did the road down to the river, which was an earthy-coloured and smooth-as-glass body of water on one side of the bridge and quick-moving on the other. From here it's possible to walk up to the elegant structures that I spied earlier from the opposite hill—one a former palace and now a sanatorium, the other a castle with an equally impressive pedigree to that in the town proper. Even the woods hold a special place in Latvian consciousness, for it is here that an epic story of love and betrayal—"the Rose of Turaida," a staple of classrooms up and down the country—reaches its tragic climax when the heroine of the story is struck down by a jilted admirer in a local cave. It was the perfect spot to simply while away the time.

Strangely enough, given Sigulda's impeccable historic and cultural credentials it's also fast becoming Latvia's adventure sports capital, a sideline first kicked off when a cable car was slung across the valley to the sanatorium at Krimulda in the 1960s. This serene mode of transport, which hummed gently as it passed by overhead at the bridge, now offers bungee jumps at the mid-way point above the river; sadly no one was brave enough to attempt it while I sat and watched it glide by. For lovers of high-octane thrills Sigulda has yet more surprises: a high-wire park, a summer toboggan, a bobsled track, a land-based skydive simulator: all have their home in this otherwise serene and attractive valley.

And yet, as I sat and stared at the Gauja I couldn't avoid an inescapable truth: try as I might, wherever I travelled and whatever I saw, I just couldn't stop thinking about Ruta. There would be no toboggans for me this time. I had to get back to Lithuania.

It was as if I'd never left. The smile, the hugs, the laughter; all was fresh and yet all so wonderfully familiar. In what was now firmly established as my room a whiteboard had been mocked up with "Welcome Back Keith!" written in big black letters. I thought my heart was about to melt.

It transpired that I had come back to Klaipėda at an opportune moment, for the day of my arrival also coincided with an open-air jazz festival that was to take place that evening in the centre of town. Ruta again played taxi driver, speeding us through a bustling night to a stop a short distance away from Theatre Square where the festivities were taking place. We made a small detour to meet a friend and colleague from the art gallery, and then as a trio we proceeded in the direction of the music.

The place was buzzing, a huge crowd spilling into the square in front of a stage where a band was belting out jazz numbers. The crowd was in an appreciative mood, clapping and cheering and stomping their feet as the band finished one number and commenced another. We each picked up a beer from a nearby stall and pushed our way through the throng so that we could get a better view. Now I could see that the band—drummer, saxophonist, bass guitarist and singer—were all in their fifties or sixties. They had great energy and played with an infectious enthusiasm, and as I looked at the throng around us I could see all ages present. It was all-inclusive: a party where everyone was invited and where all could enjoy themselves without fear or hindrance. What a contrast to the time in 1939 when Hitler had addressed jubilant German-speaking crowds in the very same square.

I pondered this the next day as I visited the History Museum of Lithuania Minor, in the heart of Klaipėda's Old Town not far from Theatre Square. There were a few other visitors taking in the exhibits, which provided a comprehensive overview of a region that had historically stretched from Palanga in the north to the eastern half of what is now the Russian exclave of Kaliningrad Oblast in the south. It transpired that prior to 1918 all of Lithuania Minor was part of German East Prussia, the ancestral heartland of the medieval Prussian state that was nevertheless home to a substantial number of ethnic Lithuanians. These Lithuanian-Prussians were also largely Protestant, in stark contrast to the inhabitants of Lithuania Major who were almost entirely Roman Catholic. In today's parlance, however, Lithuania Minor is generally restricted to the lands immediately around Klaipėda—the former Memelland—and the museum's modest collection of black-and-white photographs testifies to the upheaval that rocked this small corner of the Baltics in the twentieth century: first Lithuania's seizure of the port in 1923 and later Hitler's triumphant return of Memel to German hands on the eve of World War II.

But I was also fascinated by the museum's documentation of the region's pagan past, particularly a scale model of a nearby sanctuary: an ancient structure that astounded archaeologists with its high degree of astronomical knowledge. Just like at the Devil Museum in Kaunas, Lithuania's modern Christian culture suddenly seemed like a mere veneer on the surface of a much older belief system. And just as the Orthodox Church was witnessing a resurgence in post-Soviet Russia, it was clear that forty-five years of atheist Communist administration had failed to stamp out the spiritual need for religion that had existed here for centuries.

The concert the night before had been great fun, and yet this wasn't the only cultural offering to be had that weekend. Before we'd parted ways and I'd hit the museum, Ruta and I had gone to a poetry recital in a local library. I didn't understand a word, but it didn't matter; the speaker's emotion was clear from the delivery, a voice of sadness tinged with regret.

Later that afternoon we reconvened at the very same warehouse that the fashion show had taken place in just a couple of weeks before. This time we weren't here to check out the latest trends; instead, a jam session was taking place and in complete contrast to the raucousness of the night before, acoustic musicians were going it unplugged. Ruta and I took up a couple of seats near the front, sitting in silence and content to both watch the performance and simply enjoy the moment.

It was as we made our way home that I mentioned the idea of crossing the short stretch of water to the Curonian Spit, that thin sliver of land that had beckoned so enticingly from Klaipėda's shore when Kristina and I first explored the night city. I'd heard so many good things about it—golden beaches, Sahara-style sand dunes, pretty towns once popular with hordes of holidaying pre-war Germans—and on a map it looked even more alluring. At just a shade under sixty miles in length it's one of the longest examples of a sand spit in the world, a unique ecological environment and a UNESCO World Heritage Site to boot.

"It is a lovely place," Ruta confirmed as we pulled into her apartment complex. "I've been there many times and know it very well. Sometimes we go there to relax with friends or with family; it's one of the best things about living in Klaipėda. Perhaps we can go together—wait one moment, let me just make a call."

It was the second time that I'd been on a boat since the crossing from Helsinki to Tallinn but that initial crossing had been in a completely different league: back then a huge behemoth had taken several hours to spirit hundreds of us across the Gulf of Finland. Here things were far more sedate, a tiny ferry taking barely ten minutes to glide across the narrow channel that connects the Curonian Lagoon with the Baltic Sea. Most people didn't even bother to get out of their cars, but I couldn't stop myself from standing by the edge to watch the seagulls fly alongside us as the forested coastline of the spit edged closer. Ruta joined me too, the wind whipping her long hair behind her.

As we docked a large sign with a detailed map of the entire Lithuanian section of the spit welcomed us to the Kuršių Nerija National Park, established shortly after independence to protect the unique ecosystems of the Curonian region. Interestingly, "Nerija" comes from "Neringa" who, according to ancient myth, was a child sea giant who formed the spit while playing on the seashore. Geographers have a much more prosaic explanation, however: it was built up over thousands of years in a process known as longshore drift, where wind- and wave-driven sand was dumped in a thin band across the entrance of the Nemunas Delta, closing it off from the open sea in the process. Whatever the truth—and I preferred the sea giant version—the statistics are undeniably impressive. Stretching from the Sambian Peninsula in the south all the way to its tip opposite Klaipėda on the mainland, the spit ranges in width from around four hundred metres at its narrowest point to just over two miles at its widest. Curiously for such an explicitly singular landform it is also partitioned politically: the northern section is Lithuanian soil, whilst the south is part of the Kaliningrad Oblast—an integral part of the Russian Federation. The spit isn't therefore simply divided between two neighbouring states; this sliver of grass and sand is now on the new frontline between the European West and the Russian East.

Yet in many ways the story of Kaliningrad crystallises the complex movement of cultures, languages and peoples that so characterise this region. Once inhabited by Sambians—speakers of the old Baltic language, ancestor of modern Latvian and Lithuanian—the indigenous people gradually became assimilated into German culture after being conquered by the Teutonic Knights in the seventeenth century. The area subsequently became the core of Germanic Prussia, the state that would eventually become the dominant force within the fragmented German lands and which Prussia itself would unite under its leadership in 1871.

During this time the city of Königsberg, as Kaliningrad was then known, flourished both as an important port and as an intellectual and cultural centre, the residence of such titans of German culture as Immanuel Kant, Käthe

Kollwitz, Agnes Miegel and E. T. A. Hoffmann. It was also the easternmost city of its size in the empire, a diverse and multicultural metropolis that profoundly influenced the Lithuanian and Polish populations nearby; indeed, the first Polish translation of the New Testament was printed in the city, as well as important works in German and Lithuanian. It even spawned its own famous mathematical problem, the seven bridges of Königsberg, which challenged both academics and visitors alike to devise a route through the city that would cross each bridge once and only once—a route that was famously proved to be impossible by Swiss mathematician Leonhard Euler in 1736.

The city's fortunes began to change, however, at the end of the First World War. The creation of the "Polish Corridor" gave a newly restored Poland access to the sea, thereby cutting off East Prussia from the rest of Germany and rendering the region an exclave—a status that continues (in altered form) to this day. Things went from bad to worse following Lithuania's annexation of Memel, and during the 1930s the Nazi regime tightened its grip on the city, slowly inflicting more and more repressive measures on the Jewish population and eventually deporting them altogether.

Königsberg's isolated position on the eastern fringes of Germany also meant that it would be first in line for any Soviet invasion, and so it came to pass as the Second World War swung inexorably in favour of the Allies. In 1944 much of the historic city suffered heavy damage from

British bombing raids, and as the Red Army drew closer towards the end of the year and into the early months of 1945 many of East Prussia's German inhabitants fled westwards and by sea: an exodus that intensified as rumours of Soviet atrocities against ethnic German civilians in the border regions began to spread. Königsberg itself withstood a three-month siege, only surrendering a month before the end of the war in Europe. When it did so virtually nothing of the once-beautiful city had survived.

The new post-war order in Europe decreed the end of East Prussia as a political entity. The region's remaining German population was almost completely expelled and the territory partitioned, with the larger southern sector transferring to Poland and the north going to the Soviet Union. More population transfers would take place: in the south the Polish authorities settled their new acquisition with Poles and Ukrainians who had been forced to leave Kresy during that region's occupation and subsequent absorption by the USSR. In the new Kaliningrad—named after Mikhail Kalinin, theoretical leader of the Soviet Union in the interwar period who was in reality subordinate to Joseph Stalin—ethnic Russians were imported from the motherland and virtually all traces of its former German status were eradicated. Today, over three hundred miles from Russia proper, the Kaliningrad region is home to almost a million Russian citizens.

In some ways it's curious that such a quirk of geography ever came to pass, for when Kaliningrad was incorporated into the USSR in 1945 the border that now exists between it and Lithuania would simply have been an internal boundary within the same sovereign state. But Kaliningrad was explicitly transferred to the RSFSR—the Russian Soviet Federative Socialist Republic—as opposed to the Lithuanian SSR, for reasons that are not entirely clear; some claim that it was because the Lithuanian Communist Party committee did not want a newly implanted and ethnically homogenous Russian population within its borders. Others, on the other hand, have suggested that Stalin intentionally created the exclave to further separate the Baltic states from the West, but if this was the plan then it backfired completely: for it is Kaliningrad that is now isolated, surrounded by NATO and the European Union, although its strategic position as Russia's only ice-free Baltic Sea port and its thoroughly Russophile population means that future sovereignty is unlikely to be up for debate anytime soon.

Ruta drove us south along a beautifully wooded road that offered the occasional tantalising glimpse of the Curonian Lagoon, its placid waters stretching to the mainland that we had left just a short while before. Pop music played on the radio and I wound down the window to get some fresh air on what had turned out to be a fantastically sunny and beautiful day. Behind us the back seat was also occupied, for Ruta had brought her younger sister Ieva along for the ride too. In her mid-teens, Ieva also seemed pleased to be there, even though—as she confided to me before we'd set off—she had been to Neringa many times before.

Our first stop was in Juodkrantė, once the German village of Schwarzort which had been popular with holidaying Prussians before the First World War. It still retains much of the genteel charm from that period, and we did as our predecessors would have done: we strolled along the lagoon-front promenade, admiring the traditional buildings and the view over the waters that seemed as smooth as glass with barely a ripple disturbing its surface. The calmness of the lagoon belies the life that depends on it; despite ongoing problems with pollution its waters teem with fish, for generations providing both a livelihood for the villages along its length and a ready source of food for Juodkrantė's sizeable bird colony.

But there are more things to do in Juodkrantė than simply shoot the breeze. It was to one such place that Ruta and Ieva led me, not far from the centre of the village: an intriguing path heading into a forest, where we saw a curious wooden statue of a smiling axe-wielding woman sitting on a sign emblazoned with the words *Raganų kalnas* pointing the way through the trees. This was Juodkrantė's famous and mysterious "Hill of Witches."

It was absolutely marvellous. The hill is a wooden sculpture park that winds through wooded paths, where every turn brings a new delight. Most of the sculptures are based on Lithuanian legends and folktales, and perhaps surprisingly the park was not born post-independence but rather was founded in the late in 1970s whilst the region was firmly under Soviet rule. Full of dragons and imps and other fantastical and paganesque creatures, some of the best statues are interactive. The three of us tried them all: the throne, where we could pretend that we were some ancient king holding court, or the four-metre-high hobby horse with steps in the base to climb to the top, or the wooden seesaw that Ieva dangled from helplessly when I put my full weight down in the chair at the other end. "This is my favourite," cried Ruta as she whooshed down a slide that formed the tongue of some devilish beast. "I used to love this one as a child."

From Juodkrantė we headed farther south, along a highway lined with birch trees gripping tightly to the sandy soils all around us. I was still musing about the Hill of Witches when we passed something that wouldn't have looked out of place on a *Wicker Man* set: a stylised sun and moon built out of what looked like wood bound with straw, themselves perched on pedestals made from the same material and sited in a small inlet of the lagoon. "They're for burning," confirmed Ruta, a ritual whose heritage stretches all the way back into Lithuania's pre-Christian era.

It's possible that this was in preparation for Saint John's Day—*Joninės* in Lithuanian—where, a couple of nights after the summer solstice each year, families and friends join together to light a bonfire and stay up to celebrate the rising of the sun, often accompanied by copious amounts of booze. As well as a chance for a final knees-up before knuckling down to the tough job of collecting the harvest, Midsummer's Eve was also traditionally a fertility festival in which the fruits of nature were celebrated in all its forms and where couples would head off into the forest together in the hunt for the elusive fern flower: said to bring luck and fortune to whoever could find them. It's a festival held throughout the Baltics, predating the arrival of Christianity; the traditional getup of flower crowns and traditional clothing certainly harks back to a distant pagan past. I just hoped that they didn't imprison visitors inside the effigies as an offering to the gods.

Before long we reached a busy lay-by teeming with cars and families and another path that again seemed to disappear into the trees. But any such suggestion that this was going to be another mere forest walk was purely illusory, for before long we emerged into a wide sandy expanse of undulating dunes, patches of marram grass and breathtaking views up and down a vast swathe of the spit.

Perhaps it's here, away from the villages and the forests, that the transitory nature of this wild landscape most openly reveals itself. The dunes are impressive in scale; the highest of their kind in Europe, they run along virtually the entire length of the spit. Yet this is a fluctuating, impermanent place, with predominantly westerly winds driving the ridge of dunes slowly eastwards towards the Curonian Lagoon. Deforestation in centuries past did much to speed up this process, so much so that villages often had to relocate from generation to generation as homes and harbours succumbed to the sands. The wealth of trees that currently exists is part of a systematic attempt to halt this movement, and visitors can only walk in specific areas; other sections of the dunes are off-limits to prevent erosion. This is probably no bad thing, for as we drank in the views over a lagoon that was now so wide that the mainland had disappeared entirely a whole busload of tourists arrived from out of nowhere, walking barefoot on the hot sands. This was indeed a popular place.

The spit was also once the home of the Kuršininkai, an almost entirely extinct Baltic ethnic group who had elsewhere been thoroughly assimilated by the Germans but on the Spit had largely preserved their distinctive culture for centuries. Curiously their language was closer to Latvian than Lithuanian, thereby forming the basis for a short-lived Latvian claim over the spit at the end of the First World War. Some twenty-five years later, towards the end of the Second, the majority of Kuršininkai fled from the Red Army during the evacuation of East Prussia; those who remained behind were subsequently expelled by the Soviet Union after the war, to be replaced with Russians and Lithuanians. Some subsequently managed to return to their homes but those who did suffered widespread discrimination, and by the mid-1950s only two hundred or so lived on the spit. Never quite forgiven for their perceived German links, most of them eventually settled in Germany for good.

The cultural legacy of the Kuršininkai lives on, however, which became evident as we slowly made our way to the largest and most southerly town in the Lithuanian section of the spit, as well as being the most westerly point in the Baltic states: the charming village of Nida.

Nida is for many visitors to Lithuania the literal and metaphorical end of the line, situated as it is just a stone's throw from the Russian border. But this enchanting place—once the German settlement of Nidden—has been popular with locals and tourists alike for well over a hundred years. Painters and writers discovered the nearby dunes and wild landscapes in the late nineteenth century, and Nidden became an artists' colony, particularly popular with expressionists and poets from nearby Königsberg. Even after its transfer to Lithuania in 1923 the settlement retained its German-speaking majority and remained popular with German visitors, most notably the Nobel Prize–winning author Thomas Mann, who fell in love with the village and its setting and built a summer house there. Mann spent three summers in Nidden between 1930 and 1932, writing parts of his epic novel *Joseph and His Brothers* in between spending time walking by the lagoon and taking in the fresh salty air of the nearby Baltic Sea. Mann fled Germany when the Nazis took power and never returned to the Curonian Spit, his house eventually becoming a recreational home for officers of the Luftwaffe. These days it's a museum dedicated to Mann and his family's brief time in Nida.

Mann's summer house is a particularly pretty example of the fairy-tale-style local architecture that makes parts of the village so attractive: all picket fences, flowers and twee wooden houses that looked at first glance like they were made of wood but were in fact made of tastefully painted corrugated iron. But as we drew closer to town we took an unexpected turn, leading us instead into a kind of landscaped suburbia full of neat, small modern-looking apartment blocks. And then, without warning, we pulled up outside one and Ruta switched off the engine. "We're home!" she smiled mischievously, obviously amused at my confusion. "This is where we can stay tonight."

Now I understood the reason for the furtive telephone call the night before: she had been checking with her parents to see if it would be okay for us to stay at their Nida holiday home. Ieva laughed as we clambered out, as if to say that she had known what Ruta had been up to all along. "I have been here so many times," she teased as Ruta opened the door into one of the apartments, "but I love coming here. Everyone does."

It was hard to argue with this observation. In the immediate post-war period Nida had reverted once more into a little-visited fishing village, its tourism industry all but destroyed. Later it was rediscovered by the Soviet elite, however, and the town, along with Juodkrantė and a couple of other villages in Neringa, became a restricted holiday region reserved for Communist Party *nomenklatura* and other favoured members of Lithuania's elite. Come the fall of the USSR and Nida was once again open to all, the holiday homes of the sort in which we now found ourselves serving as a testament to Nida's enduring popularity with all and especially with Lithuanians and Germans keen to rediscover their Curonian heritage.

And Nida is indeed a magical spot. We did as Mann might once have done, gambolling along the waterfront parallel to a lagoon so still it almost looked like we could walk on its surface. The mainland was so distant by now that the sea and sky seemed to merge into one, with only an occasional glimpse of a distant treeline hinting at the possibility of a horizon. The local gang of toughs was out in force, too: a group of graceful white swans, scouting the shoreline for scraps of food.

The heritage of the Kuršininkai makes itself known in more subtle ways too. We spied *Nidden kurenwimpel* ("Curonian pennants") throughout the town: individualised and ornately carved flags particular to the local Kuršininkai families who were once resident throughout the spit. The flags often feature animal and human figures, reminiscent of a long-lost pagan writing tradition, and the local cemetery is home to several rare *krikštai*: pagan burial markers that take the place of tombstones.

We went to the Baltic too, along a short forest walk that took us from Nida proper to a far wilder coast. If the lagoon is sedate and tranquil then the Baltic is its older, brasher big brother; here there is open sea all the way to the distant shores of Scandinavia. Gales can lash this coast when the storms roll in across the water but today it was in a far calmer mood, with gentle waves lapping a fine beach of golden sand that runs the entire western edge of the spit. We sat here awhile and soaked up some rays, a quick paddle in the cool Baltic our only exertion of note.

The dunes that characterise so much of the spit are present in Nida as well. They loom over the southern edge of town like great monoliths of sand; king of these is the fifty-metre-high Parnidis Dune. We scrambled breathlessly up the path to its summit where we were greeted by a giant sundial, covered in runes like some ancient obelisk erected by people from long ago. But the real treat was the view: in one direction I could see across to Nida, where a multitude of pretty yachts bobbed in its harbour. The spit stretched off in the distance, dune and forest squeezed on both sides by water until I knew that, somewhere beyond, it would finally taper to a point opposite Klaipėda.

But it was the other direction that really captivated us. Here—just as I had done in Narva almost two months before—I was able to stare across to Russia, an ever-secret and forbidden world: elusive and fleeting, within sight but beyond reach. Yellow sands flecked with marram grass extended out towards a cloak of dark-green forest: a nature reserve that was off-limits to visitors that formed a no-man's-land just before the border itself. It was strange to think that from here, courtesy of Schengen, I could travel freely as far as Spain or Portugal without so much as a passport and yet I wouldn't be able to cross an invisible line only a couple of miles to the south: a border that throughout history had shifted as much as the great dunes that call this beautiful peninsula home.

And as the salt-tinged breeze blew softly across us I tried to contemplate what I had seen and heard and felt and learned during my time in Estonia, Latvia and Lithuania. In truth, I felt a deep joy and an aching sadness, a contradictory conflict of emotion that made me want to smile and cry all at the same time. There was the happiness of witnessing a beautiful and unique land first hand, of meeting a kind and wonderful people and of being able to gain insight into the thoughts and dreams of others who were fortunate enough to call this place home. I had come looking for the ghost of Lenin and instead I'd found a new Europe, three countries bound both to the past and to the future but that had definitively and defiantly chosen which direction they would face—even if not everyone was entirely on board.

But there was sadness too, for I knew that it would be in Nida that I would come to the end of my journey. And as Ruta and I stared over the sweeping panorama in front of us it finally occurred to me that perhaps the biggest change to have taken place since the fall of the iron curtain was the simple fact that I was allowed to be here at all. This was at least one legacy of the Soviet Union that had disappeared completely.

Postscript

∗ ∗ ∗

IN THE UPPER FLOORS OF Kaliningrad Cathedral, home to a beautifully presented museum and the restored Wallenrodt Library, is an exquisitely detailed model of Königsberg as it might have looked at the dawn of the twentieth century. Quaint little barges and wooden sailing ships line the quaysides of the Pregolya River—itself criss-crossed by the city's famous bridges—and red-tiled townhouses adjoin cobbled avenues and cosy tram-lined town squares. The model, which takes up an entire room, is dominated in the centre by the cathedral and its island, whilst a short distance away the elegant form of Königsberg Castle looms large above the city. This idyllic scene cannot fail to impress on the viewer an overwhelmingly Germanic architectural consistency that was once said to rival the likes of Prague and Krakow in its splendour.

This model is, of course, of a city that essentially no longer exists. The townhouses have long since gone, swept away in the chaos of the Second World War, and even the magnificent castle fared no better; its ruins were blown up and bulldozed by the conquering Red Army and the brutalist House of Soviets was built in its place. The cathedral too was rendered but a shell of its former self, and the numerous buildings that it once shared Kant Island with were swept away to form the open park that exists to this day. Königsberg, once a beacon of the Enlightenment, was closed and declared off-limits to foreigners.

More evidence of this destruction is presented in the cathedral's impressive nave. Lining the walls are photos from Königsberg's heyday, as well as the subsequent devastation wrought by the aerial and terrestrial bombardment that took place during the initial stages of the Allied invasion of Germany and the final push to Berlin.

The devastation enabled the Communists to remodel Königsberg in their own image, renaming the resultant creation Kaliningrad in 1946. Very little of the original city now remains: the beautiful cathedral was only rebuilt in the early 1990s thanks largely to German money, and apart from a few remaining red-brick walls, bastions and gates there is scant physical evidence to indicate that this was once an integral part of the Reich.

Indeed, walking along the traffic-choked avenue of Leninsky Prospekt to Ploshchad Pobedy—Victory Square—I was surprised by just how Russian the place felt. I had wondered if the region's isolation from the motherland or the immediate proximity of its Polish and Lithuanian neighbours might have had some sort of moderating effect, but no. The buildings, the trolley buses, the flags, the street signs, the people: all were undeniably Russian. I might as well have been strolling around Moscow or Irkutsk or Nizhny Novgorod. Perhaps the only real difference was that even though it was the depths of winter the temperature was still above freezing, a climate those citizens stranded in the Russian capital could surely only dream of.

I was staying—where else?—in a Khrushcheby, the home of a friend of a man named Dima whom I'd met via couchsurfing. He was a friendly chap, not much younger than me and with good English for someone who had never travelled outside Russia. Unusually I wasn't actually staying with him, a situation I didn't readily appreciate until we had arrived at the apartment after a long trudge through town. It was already late, my bus from Gdańsk having taken much longer than anticipated, and as we climbed to the top floor he explained that his domestic situation didn't lend itself well to hosting but that his contact wouldn't mind me staying at his place. "And do they know that I'm staying here? Is anyone going to turn up in the middle of the night to ask what I'm doing here?" I pondered as he passed me the key.

"Oh, it's absolutely fine, my friend is now living with his girlfriend." He smiled reassuringly as we said our farewells: "He is happy to let you stay here. Good luck."

I spent the rest of the following day exploring the city. In addition to the cathedral I took in the Bunker Museum—the hideout of the German Command during the final siege of the city—and the grandiose Victory Park, replete with eternal flame and memorials to those who paid the ultimate sacrifice in the fight against the Nazi menace. I pretended to walk on the ceiling at the whimsical Upside-Down House and explored the excellent Museum of the World Ocean, where an enthusiastic former crewmember gave me a personal tour of *Submarine B-413*. It was hard to imagine how up to eighty men would spend weeks living and working together in such cramped conditions. I even spotted a couple of Soviet-era tanks casually decorating the streets, a reminder of the strife that created the Kaliningrad of today.

Shortly afterwards I took a car out to Kurshskaya Kosa National Park, located on the southern half of the fabled Curonian Spit. It took little more than an hour from the capital, just a brief stop at Zelenogradsk (once the spa town of Kranz) and a payment of a few hundred roubles at the park entrance and then I was finally back on that magical sliver of land separating the chilly Baltic from the still waters of the Curonian Lagoon. The landscape was just as I remembered it from the Lithuanian side: tall wild grass-covered dunes, thick forests of pine and wide sandy beaches, occasionally interrupted by quaint villages once known by different names: Lesnoy (Sarkau), Rybachy (Rossitten), Morskoye (Pilkoppen). But unlike its northern counterpart I pretty much had the place to myself, and as I made my way farther north I took the time to stop and breathe in this marvellous, primordial landscape.

I had often wondered how the partitioning of this unique landform came into being, and it transpires that it had nothing to do with the Soviets. At the end of the First World War the powers that be decided that German land to the north of the Nemunas River would be administered by the League of Nations, pending a final decision on the area's future: the district of Memelland that was subsequently annexed by Lithuania. The spit is simply divided at the same latitude as the mouth of the Nemunas on the mainland.

Such a division meant, of course, that barely twenty five miles into the park came the border that shuts off Kaliningrad from the outside world. This would be my end of the road; with my hire car and single-entry visa there would be no way back if I chose to proceed. And so I turned around and headed back to the big city, content that I had spent some time in such a special place but also saddened that I was unable to enjoy it in its entirety. It had been a good visit.

But it was the "Russianness" of it all, if I may call it that, that really struck me about Kaliningrad and its eponymous oblast. Here the policy of Russification had been put into overdrive; those Germans who did not die or flee in the face of the Soviet onslaught were rounded up and deported *en masse*. In its place an outpost of the USSR was created down to the minutest detail and a Russian population implanted to make the region's ethnic and cultural transformation irreversible. It was strange to think that every single person living in Kaliningrad today could claim a local heritage going back no more than a couple of generations at most. The Estonians, Latvians and Lithuanians who would protest at length about the impact of Russification on their national and cultural integrity really have nothing on the native Germans of Königsberg, who must have known that they would never again be able to call the Baltic home. The extant statue of Lenin, still standing proud not far from Kaliningrad's main bus station, is but a testament to the completeness of that transformation and of a people whose time has come to pass.

B I B L I O G R A P H Y

Bird, Tim. 1999. *A Baltic Odyssey: Exploring the Baltic Sea Region.* Taifuuni.

Bojtár, Endre. 1999. *Forward to the Past: A Cultural History of the Baltic States.* Central European University Press.

Bousfield, Jonathan. 2011. *The Rough Guide to Estonia, Latvia and Lithuania.* Rough Guides.

Buzayev, Vladimir. 2013. *Legal and Social Situation of the Russian-Speaking Minority in Latvia.* Averti-R, Ltd.

Buzayev, Vladimir, et al. 2011. *Citizens of a Non-Existent State.* Averti-R, Ltd.

Egremont, Max. 2012. *Forgotten Land: Journeys among the Ghosts of East Prussia.* Picador.

European Commission against Racism and Intolerance (ECRI). 2012. *ECRI Report on Latvia: Fourth Monitoring Cycle.*

Ezergailis, Andrew. 1996. *The Holocaust in Latvia 1941–1944.* Historical Institute of Latvia.

Hatherley, Owen. 2015. *Landscapes of Communism: A History through Buildings.* Penguin Books.

Hiden, John, and Patrick Salmon. 1991. *The Baltic Nations and Europe: Estonia, Latvia and Lithuania in the Twentieth Century.* Longman.

Hiden, John, et al. 2009. *The Baltic Question during the Cold War.* Routledge.

Jacobsson, Bengt. 2009. *The European Union and the Baltic States: Changing Forms of Governance.* Routledge.

Jones, Griff. 2005. *To the Baltic with Bob.* Penguin Books.

Kasekamp, Andres. 2010. *A History of the Baltic States.* Palgrave Macmillan.

Lane, Thomas, et al. 2013. *The Baltic States: Estonia, Latvia and Lithuania.* Routledge.

Lieven, Anatol. 1993. *The Baltic Revolution: Estonia, Latvia, Lithuania and the Path to Independence.* Yale University Press.

Mitrofanovs, Miroslavs, et al. 2006. *The Last Prisoners of the Cold War: The Stateless People of Latvia in Their Own Words.* Averti-R, Ltd.

Palmer, Alan. 2006. *The Baltic: A New History of the Region and Its People.* Overlook Press.

Plakans, Andrejs. 2011. *A Concise History of the Baltic States.* Cambridge University Press.

Presser, Brandon, et al. 2012. *Estonia, Latvia and Lithuania.* Lonely Planet.

Prevost, Dyranda, and Natalia Dushkina. 1999. *Living Places in Russia.* The Images.

Purs, Aldis. 2012. *Baltic Facades: Estonia, Latvia and Lithuania since 1945.* Reaktion Books.

Richmond, Simon, et al. 2015. *Russia.* Lonely Planet.

About the Author

∗ ∗ ∗

KEITH RUFFLES IS ORIGINALLY FROM London but grew up in various towns and cities across the United Kingdom; today he is a civil servant based in Belfast who dreams of packing it all in to travel the world instead. Keith earned both an MSc and a BSc in geography from the University of Leicester and is interested in everything from politics, religion, and current affairs to the environment and animal rights; his work has been published in a number of national newspapers and magazines. He has already travelled to seven former Soviet states and is the first person in his family to have visited North Korea.

Baltic Lenin is his first book.

11574723R00170

Printed in Great Britain
by Amazon